HEIDEGGER, BEING, AND TRUTH

HEIDEGGER,
BEING,
AND TRUTH

by LASZLO VERSÉNYI

New Haven and London, Yale University Press
1965

Copyright © 1965 by Yale University.
Designed by Crimilda Pontes,
set in Times Roman type,
and printed in the United States of America by
the Carl Purington Rollins Printing-Office
of the Yale University Press.
Distributed in Canada by McGill University Press.
All rights reserved. This book may not be
reproduced, in whole or in part, in any form
(except by reviewers for the public press),
without written permission from the publishers.

Library of Congress catalog card number: 65–11189

Published with assistance from the
Louis Stern Memorial Fund.

TO CHARLES W. HENDEL
PROFESSOR EMERITUS

ACKNOWLEDGMENTS

I am indebted to Professor George A. Schrader for reading most of the manuscript and offering valuable criticism.

Thanks are due to Williams College for granting me leave and financial aid to complete this study; also to the American Council of Learned Societies and the American Philosophical Society for their supporting grants.

To my friend Leonard W. Conversi I owe a debt for editing the manuscript and eliminating from it the worst offenses against the English language.

Last but not least I would like to thank Professor Charles W. Hendel who, more than a dozen years ago, assisted at the birth and supervised the early growth of this study, and ever since has followed its development with friendly interest. For this, and for many another act of kindness, this book is gratefully dedicated to him.

LASZLO VERSÉNYI

Williamstown, Massachusetts
December 1964

CONTENTS

Abbreviations   x

1. Existence and Truth: The Concept of Truth in
   Being and Time   1
       Problem and Method   1
       Existence as World-Disclosure   9
       Disclosure as the Essence of Truth   33
       Excursus   43

2. Humanism, Subjectivism, Nihilism   52
       Plato's Theory of Truth   54
       The Cartesian World-View   60
       The Kantian Critique   63
       Nietzsche's Metaphysics   68
       Being and Time *as Metaphysics*   74

3. Truth and Being   86
       Truth and Freedom   86
       Truth and Art   91
       Truth and Nature   105
       Truth and Thought   108
       Truth and Man   126
       Truth and the Word   132
       Truth Needs Men   136
       Waiting for Truth   142

4. Beyond Philosophy   159
       Beyond Metaphysics   159
       Beyond Good and Evil   176

Index   199

ABBREVIATIONS OF WORKS BY MARTIN HEIDEGGER

Ar   *Vom Wesen und Begriff der physis. Arist.* Phys. *B 1*
(Milano-Varese, Istituto editoriale cisalpino, 1960). *Of
the Essence and Concept of Physis in Aristotle's* Physics
B 1

BT   *Sein und Zeit* (6th ed. Tuebingen, Neomarius, 1949),
Eng. trans. John Macquarrie and Edward Robinson,
Being and Time* (New York, Harper, 1962).

E   *Erlaeuterungen zu Hoelderlins Dichtung* (Frankfurt am
Main, Klostermann, 1951). *Hoelderlin Interpretations*

ED   *Aus der Erfahrung des Denkens* (Pfullingen, Neske,
1954). *Out of the Experience of Thought*

Einf   *Einfuehrung in die Metaphysik* (Tuebingen, Niemeyer,
1953). *Introduction to Metaphysics*

FD   *Die Frage nach dem Ding* (Tuebingen, Niemeyer, 1962).
The Question of the Thing

G   *Vom Wesen des Grundes* (3d ed. Frankfurt am Main,
Klostermann). *Of the Essence of the Ground*

*In all double page references to *Sein und Zeit* (e.g. 42/56) the
first number refers to the 6th ed., the second to the Macquarrie-
Robinson translation. (All translations in this book are, however,
the author's.)

Gel   *Gelassenheit* (Pfullingen, Neske, 1959).

Holzw *Holzwege* (2d ed. Frankfurt am Main, Klostermann). *Paths in the Wood*

Hum   *Ueber den Humanismus* (Frankfurt am Main, Klostermann, 1949). *Letter on Humanism*

Id   *Identitaet und Differenz* (Pfullingen, Neske, 1957). *Identity and Difference*

KP   *Kant und das Problem der Metaphysik* (2d ed. Frankfurt am Main, Klostermann, 1951). *Kant and the Problem of Metaphysics*

KTh   *Kants These ueber das Sein* (Frankfurt am Main, Klostermann, 1963). *Kant's Sentence about Being*

N   *Nietzsche* I, II (Pfullingen, Neske, 1961).

PLW   *Platons Lehre von der Wahrheit* (Bern, Francke, 1942). *Plato's Theory of Truth*

SG   *Der Satz vom Grund* (Pfullingen, Neske, 1957). *Nothing Is without Ground*

U   *Unterwegs zur Sprache* (Pfullingen, Neske, 1959). *Toward Language*

Vortr *Vortraege und Aufsaetze* (Pfullingen, Neske, 1954). *Lectures and Essays*

WhD   *Was heisst Denken* (Tuebingen, Niemeyer, 1954). *Thought*

WiM   *Was ist Metaphysik* (5th ed. Frankfurt am Main, Klostermann, 1949). *What Is Metaphysics*

WW   *Vom Wesen der Wahrheit* (2d ed. Frankfurt am Main, Klostermann, 1949). *Of the Essence of Truth*

1.
EXISTENCE AND TRUTH:
THE CONCEPT OF TRUTH
IN *BEING AND TIME*

Problem and Method

From the beginnings of Western thought, the problems of
Being and Truth have been interrelated. Heidegger's conception of Truth may be as different as possible from those
of his predecessors, but in this respect he does not deviate
from the tradition. Being and Truth are inseparable and, in
the end, interchangeable terms in his philosophy.

The central problem of Heidegger's thought is the problem of Being. "To think of Being" is, according to him, the
purpose of philosophy, and he therefore proposes, at the
very beginning of *Being and Time,* to direct all his efforts
toward reviving the "battle of the giants about Being"
(Plato, *Sophist* 244A) which much of Western thought,
oblivious of its purpose, allowed to lapse. Since Being and
Truth are thus closely related in his thought, Heidegger's
ontological investigations will necessarily give us insight
into his conception of Truth. In the following, I shall, accordingly, give an account of the first stage of his inquiry
into Being in *Being and Time*.

1

Heidegger is well aware of the fact that there are many obstacles in the way of such an investigation. Being is "the most universal" concept (Aristotle, *Metaphysics* B, 4, 1001a, 21), an understanding of which is included in whatsoever we apprehend (Aquinas, *Summa Theol.*, 2.2, qu. 94. art. 2). But the universality of this concept is not that of a genus, for Being transcends all genera; it is "transcendent par excellence." Consequently it cannot be defined in terms of its lowest genus and its specific differences—it seems to be an indefinite and undefinable concept. It does not even appear that there is any need for a definition of Being, for in all our knowing and asserting we seem to understand what we mean when we use the verb "to be" in all its forms. The meaning of Being seems "self-evident."

Far from proving the pointlessness of his inquiry, however, these objections indicate to Heidegger only that Being, the most universal notion, is conceptually the most obscure and problematic one. It is so "immediately self-evident" that its mediate, conceptual understanding is for us the hardest thing to attain to. Indeed, the question, "What is Being?" is not merely unanswered, but is so obscure and undirected that we do not even know where to turn for an answer and in what manner an answer should be given. Therefore, a clarification of the question itself must constitute the first step in any investigation of Being.

Every inquiry has three constitutive moments: (a) the object of inquiry, i.e. that which is in question, (b) the subject of the inquiry, i.e. that which is interrogated, asked about what is in question, and (c) a conceptual framework within which the answer could be formulated and given, an explicit theoretical intention that could be fulfilled.

In this particular investigation, that which is in question (a) is Being. This seems to present no immediate problem, for we do have a vague, preconceptual grasp of the meaning of the term when we use it in everyday discourse. But (b)

Being is everywhere. Every being participates in it and can thus be questioned as to its mode of Being, and this is what makes our inquiry difficult: it is not by virtue of a lack of possible directions, a scarcity of beings to be interrogated, that our questioning is undirected, but rather by their over-abundance. As to the conceptual framework (c) within which the answer could be given, the manner in which a satisfactory solution to the problem could be formulated, we are in an even greater quandary. A categorical explanation applies to all beings. But Being transcends all genera. How is it to be conceived?

To get out of these difficulties Heidegger takes a step which has far-reaching consequences for the whole of his investigation of Being in *Being and Time:*

We want to clarify our inquiry by exploring and developing the question, "What is Being?," along the lines set forth, but, he points out, questioning with all the constitutive moments (a, b, c) to be analyzed is itself the mode of Being of a particular kind of being, the being we are ourselves: man. Therefore, developing and unfolding the question itself, we are already involved in investigating man, the questioner, as to his Being. The clarification of our question amounts to an inquiry into the mode of Being of that being whose characteristic mode of being is to be concerned and to raise questions. The explicit elaboration of the question of Being requires a preliminary analysis of the mode of Being of Dasein.[1] Ontology proper, the investigation of Being, must be preceded by "fundamental ontology," the investigation of man's existence.

---

1. *Dasein* is Heidegger's term, in his early writings, for man. Combining *da:* here, there, with *sein:* to be, being, the traditional meaning of the word is: existence, presence, life, but Heidegger uses it only in reference to human existence. As the word has, by now, become a *terminus technicus,* I shall leave it untranslated in this study.

One might ask at this point whether it is possible to engage in this investigation without moving in an obvious circle. Can one define the Being of one particular being without first raising the question as to the meaning of Being itself? Are we not presupposing in the analysis of the Being of Dasein precisely that to which this analysis is supposed to lead? To Heidegger, such objections have no force. The proposed inquiry is not circular at all, he asserts, because the mode of Being of any being can be defined without our having an explicit definition of the meaning of Being as such. That this is so is obvious from the fact that definitions of the first kind are generally available while the precise meaning of Being is still unknown. What our inquiry pre-supposes is a vague, preconceptual understanding of Being, and this is something that we the questioners undoubtedly possess. But that is not at all what the inquiry ultimately aims at—an explicit conceptual grasp of Being—and so the end is by no means presupposed here. Indeed, the investigation cannot be circular at all, because it is not a deductive proof from presuppositions *we make,* but the unfolding of a structure that *we are,* the analysis of a mode of Being—that of Dasein—that is given with our own existence.

This is exactly what makes the inquiry of special concern to us. The fundamental problem of ontology, that to which an analysis of the mode of Being of Dasein is preliminary, is the problem of Being. This problem must be faced if ontology is to be a living philosophy. But whether or not ontology survives is not a question of merely theoretical interest, for ontology is the highest manifestation of the "humanity" of human beings. Man is, above all, the onto-logical animal, i.e. the being whose mode of Being is to be concerned about the Being in which it participates. Its nature consists in the fact that it has an understanding of and essential relation to its own Being. Dasein *is* in such a way that, in its Being, its own Being is always already disclosed to it. Heidegger calls this relation to and disclosure of Being "existence," and it is in this sense that the sentence "the essence of Dasein lies in its existence" is to be understood.

In order that Dasein merely exist in some manner, the ontological structure of existence need not be transparent to it. Ontically, factually, Dasein is characterized by existence even if it has no explicit conceptual understanding of its Being. This is an average, commonplace, "existential" (*existenziell*) grasp of existence. But an ontological, "existentialistic" (*existenzial*) understanding means a thematic disclosure of "existentiality," i.e. of the ontological structure of existence. This is what fundamental ontology, the existentialistic analysis, aims at, and according to Heidegger this is the only kind of disclosure that fully unfolds and realizes Dasein's potentialities and thereby fulfills its existence. Since the essence of Dasein lies in its existence, an existentialistic analysis is nothing else than the radicalization of a certain mode of questioning which essentially belongs to the mode of Being of Dasein as an ontological being. Fundamental ontology is therefore neither a purely theoretical nor an arbitrary pursuit: it is but an intensification of our own mode of Being. Engaging in it we only engage ourselves deliberately in what we are already engaged in by our nature (as ontological beings).

This extreme involvement of Dasein in our inquiry into Being—that both the questioning and that which is in question are our own mode of Being—should be an impulse rather than a deterrent in our investigation. The fact that the problem of Being inevitably involves us, that merely by raising the question, "What is Being?," we are ourselves in question as to our own Being, manifests that the investigation is our proper study and essential task. It shows, furthermore, that we, the questioners, have a preeminent

relation to what is in question here (Being), and are therefore
eminently suited to be the subject interrogated (b) about its
Being. If our involvement makes the investigation circular,
our task is not to avoid the circle but to get into it so that
it can be illuminated from within.

Having anchored his investigation of Being in an existentialistic analysis of Dasein, Heidegger has solved the problem of clarifying the second constitutive element (b) in the
inquiry, i.e. what particular being will be interrogated about
Being. He now has to find (c) the right method for conduct-
ing his investigation.

Adopting the method of phenomenology, Heidegger
emphasizes that the selection of this method does not subject
the inquiry to a certain limited point of view. Phenomenology
rightly understood is not a philosophical doctrine or point
of view at all. It is a mere method specifying the way in
which the investigation is to be conducted without prejudice
to its subject matter. To explain what he means by phenomenology Heidegger presents an analysis of the two words,
phainomenon and *logos,* combined in it.

The Greek *phainomenon,* derived from the verb *phainesthai* (to appear, to show itself), refers to that which shows
itself, is apparent, is disclosed, open to sight. A phenomenon is thus anything that shows itself, anything that is, or
can be, brought to light. (*Phos,* the Greek word for light, has
the same root as *phaino,* to bring to light, to show, and
phainesthai.) In this sense *phainomena* can be, and occasionally have been, identified with *ta onta,* i.e. whatever is
in any way, any being whatsoever. Another sense of phenomenon is mere seeming; the word here refers to that
which seems to be something it is not. But this negative
connotation of phenomenon presupposes the first, positive
meaning, and is but a privative modification of it.

Both senses of the word are to be distinguished from what
we call "appearance," for an appearance (*Erscheinung*) is,

for Heidegger, precisely that which is only indicated by certain signs but does not appear itself. The symptoms of a disease indicate the disease, but in all such manifestations of the disease it is not the disease itself which appears; only signs show themselves and by showing themselves make apparent that—the disease—which itself is never open to sight. The appearance (the disease) is not to be seen; it is manifested by phenomena (the symptoms) that appear but are not appearances in the sense in which Heidegger defines the word.

There is a further, related sense of the word, the Kantian one, in which a phenomenon is that which appears in objective experience, and, by presenting itself, hides something that can never be apprehended (the noumena). This use of "phenomenon" Heidegger calls the everyday or common-sense use, and he limits the phenomenological use of the concept to connoting that which, in a Kantian system of reference, is apprehended concomitantly with common-sense phenomena but is not itself the content of apprehension. The transcendental horizons of experience in Kant— pure forms of intuition and concepts of the understanding— within which common-sense phenomena must appear but which themselves are never common-sense phenomena (the a priori conditions of the possibility of experience, which are manifested by but are not themselves objects of experience) are what Heidegger calls the phenomena of phenomenology.

The Greek *logos* has also received a variety of interpretive translations in traditional philosophy. Discourse, reason, thought, concept, ground, definition, judgment, etc. are so many words for *logos*. For Heidegger the function of *logos* as discourse is *deloun:* the disclosure of what the *logos* is about. Aristotle had explained this function of *logos* as *apophansis:* logos reveals something, namely that about which the speaker speaks, to the speaker and his interlocutors. *Logos* as *apophansis* exposes, uncovers, lays open to sight, reveals. This is why it can be "true" in the literal sense of the Greek *alethes:* it discloses (*aletheuei*) something, brings it from hiddenness (*letheia*) to light, to disclosure (*aletheia*). This is also why it can be "false" (*pseudos*) inasmuch as it fails to reveal, or even hides, by disclosing something as that which it is not.

If we compare the above meanings of phenomenon (that which is disclosed) and *logos* (that which discloses) the inner relation of what is designated by these words combined in the name phenomenology is apparent. Phenomenology, in Heidegger's Greek, means *legein ta phainomena,* or, since *legein* means *apophainesthai, apophainesthai ta phainomena:* to disclose that which shows itself on its own as it shows itself on its own. This is the maxim of modern phenomenology: "to the things themselves."

Phenomenology is thus a method which—without influencing the subject matter investigated—demands a direct approach and an unbiased openness toward that which may reveal itself in the investigation. It is pristine disclosure or unprejudiced description. Its antithesis is prescription or constructive interpretation, which construes its subject matter within and on the basis of a preconceived system or project.

Now if phenomenology means this openness toward whatever may reveal itself and if the phenomenon proper of phenomenology is for Heidegger whatever does not directly become a common-sense phenomenon—e.g. the Kantian conditions of the possibility of experience—but reveals itself concomitantly with or antecedent to common-sense phenomena, then phenomenology is eminently fit to be the method with which to investigate what ontology is concerned about: the Being of beings, which, as the phenomenon proper of phenomenology, reveals itself in and through common-sense phenomena (beings), discloses itself unthematically, and is understood preconceptually, without ever becoming itself a mere phenomenon (being) in all our experience. In other words, for Heidegger, phenomenology proper is ontology, or, what is to say the same, ontology is possible only as phenomenology. Phenomenology and ontology are accordingly not two disciplines—among others—of philosophy, but, rather, these names characterize philosophy proper with respect to its subject matter (Being) and its method (openness toward that which reveals itself as the source of all revelation). Since ontology begins as fundamental ontology—the existentialistic analysis of Dasein—our phenomenological approach will be hermeneutic: an interpretation, exposition, and explanation of Dasein's existence to Dasein itself, an unfolding of Dasein's understanding of Being.

Existence as World-Disclosure

In the existentialistic analysis of Dasein, we are in question ourselves. We are the questioners, we are interrogated as to our own Being, and the questioning itself is but a radicalization of our existence. Heidegger's preliminary characterization of Dasein can be given as follows:

"The essence of Dasein lies in its existence" (*BT* 42/56): in its openness toward, awareness of, confrontation with, and concern for its own Being. This means that the "what" (*essentia*) of Dasein must be understood on the basis of its "that": on the basis of its disclosure to itself *that* it is and has to be. The characteristics of Dasein are not objective qualities of a lifeless substance but modes of Being transparent to Dasein as its own possibilities. Dasein is essentially a possibility to itself, i.e. not an unselfconscious substantial entity of fixed objective properties, but a being to which its own modes of Being are revealed as a demand rather than a fact, as what it has to be rather than what it actually is. Dasein does not "exist" first as a substance to which it can

then relate itself in a contemplative third-person relationship (such a relationship is, for Heidegger, but a degenerate,
derivative mode of self-relation), but it is always already
related to itself as something to be achieved, something at
stake. Dasein is for and through itself what it has to be.
Since its modes of Being are always revealed to Dasein as
"its own," it can accept and fulfill them, it can decide to be
what it has to be, or it can refuse to make this decision and
try to ignore and escape what it has to be. It can project
itself into its possibilities, face and realize them, i.e. ac-
knowledge and meet their challenge as "its own," in which
case Dasein exists "authentically," or it can fail to do so.
"Unauthentic existence" is an ontologically deficient mode
of existence because unauthentic Dasein fails to understand
its Being as its own. Nevertheless unauthentic Dasein is
still an ontological being for it is still concerned about its
Being in some way, e.g. in the manner of trying to flee from
it. As, in the biblical view of man, he can have a negative
relation to God (in sin) while at the same time it is impossible
for him, whose essence lies in his God-relationship, not to be
related to God at all, so in Heidegger's view of existence
there is a deficient mode of "being ontological," but not to
be ontological at all is impossible to Dasein, whose essence
lies in its existence, i.e. in its concern about Being.

As long as Dasein exists it is characterized by a mode of
Being called Being-in-the-world. Heidegger's use of this
hyphenated term indicates that we are dealing here with a
unitary, organic, structural whole whose elements, though
amenable to analysis, cannot be altogether separated from
each other, and, if isolated, would lose not only whatever
organic function they had within the whole but, quite likely,
all meaning and function altogether. To say that Dasein is
always characterized by Being-in-the-world means not only
that Dasein is always involved in a great variety of essential
relationships with all sorts of other beings without which

(relationships) it could not exist, but also that these beings and the world itself are dependent for their mode of Being on Dasein's relations to them. They too would not be what they are but for these relationships, which are thus essential not only to Dasein but also to everything in its world.

The structural moments into which Being-in-the-world may be analyzed are: 1. the world that worldly Dasein is in, 2. the being whose mode of Being is to be-in-the-world, and 3. the Being-in or in-dwelling of Dasein as Being-in-the-world. This Being-in, as we shall see, is not a spatial relation, although it is, among other things, the basis of all spatial relations. In Heidegger's use the term (*In-sein*) refers to Dasein's intentionality, its interest in (*inter-esse*), awareness of, openness toward, familiarity and involvement with the beings in its world. Being-in characterizes Dasein as its own, and the world's, inner light, enlightenment, and illumination, without which neither Dasein nor its world would be "there," i.e. disclosed, illuminated, and apparent-transparent. Being-in stands for disclosure, discovery, or revelation as an essential structural moment of Dasein's Being-in-the-world.

1. Heidegger's analysis of "world" and "worldliness" does not depart from the originally planned existentialistic analysis of Dasein. "World" in Heidegger does not designate an aggregate or totality of all things in the universe; it is a characteristic of Dasein, and "worldliness" is an ontological concept for one of Dasein's "existentialia" (necessary modes of Being). Ontic beings (those not characterized by a concern about Being) are not worldly; they merely belong in the world, while world essentially belongs to Dasein (in the double sense that worldliness is an essential quality of Dasein and Dasein-relatedness is an essential quality of all beings in the world).

The beings Dasein encounters in the world are other

ontological, i.e. worldly, beings like Dasein, or they are
ontic beings. Dasein's concern about ontic and ontological
beings and their mode of Being constitutes Dasein's worldliness. This concern comprehends all forms of worldly relations: caring for, taking care of, being interested in, aware
of, using, employing, handling, etc., as well as not caring
about, neglecting, ignoring, being indifferent to, etc. Ontic
beings fall into two categories. They are either "merely
present" (*vorhanden*) or "at hand" and "of use" (*zuhanden*).
"Merely present" are the things Dasein contemplates ab-
stractly and theoretically, as it were, without having any
immediate practical interest in them, while "at hand" are
the beings Dasein discovers in practical circumspection,
i.e. in view of a purpose for which they could be of use.
Utensils (*Zuhandene*) are not simply there (*vorhanden,*
existent in the traditional sense of the word) first and, after-
wards, discovered as also useful, but are discovered right
at the beginning as utensils. The south wind is not noticed
as present first and then made use of, but is originally
discovered in view of its usefulness to agriculture and sailing
and its harmfulness to housing. In fact, not only are utensils
not discovered as mere things first and then employed for
our purposes, but nothing ever is discovered as "merely
there" (*vorhanden*), because Dasein's discovery of ontic
beings is always guided by a practical intent or purpose.
Originally, Dasein views ontic beings exclusively as *pragmata* or *chremata* in the literal sense, as something belonging to our *praxis,* defined by our *chresis* (use, employment),
and appropriate or inappropriate to our *chreia* (service,
need, want, etc.).[2] The first moment of encounter is always
evaluation. In this evaluation, *pragmata* may eventually
turn out to be useless and their uselessness may reveal

2. Heidegger's term *Zuhandenes* is very nearly a literal translation of *chrema* (derived from *cheir,* hand) and has all its original
connotations.

their mere obtrusive presence. But it is only when a utensil thwarts Dasein's purposive search or practical activity by its striking uselessness that Dasein becomes aware of the fact that it is "there" (*vorhanden*). "Utensil" and "mere thing" are not terms for different kinds of ontic beings; they designate different relations of Dasein to them. That which on account of its temporary uselessness is being regarded now as merely present might be found useful again, i.e. might turn into a utensil at a later time. And the same thing can happen in reverse. The mere objective presence of a thing is not noticed as long as it functions well. *Pragmata* are inconspicuous and one is hardly aware of their being there at all. One is not particularly conscious of the pen one writes with as long as it does write. But when the smooth functioning of a utensil is disturbed, its presence becomes obtrusive. We become aware of it "being there" to no purpose.

Dasein's discovery of ontic beings is always purposive, aim-directed, teleological in the traditional language of philosophy. Moreover, even when *pragmata* have already been discovered, it is a functional-teleological connection that relates them to each other. They are what they are only within a system of functional reference: a hammer serves for hammering, hammering for building a house, the house for the protection of either man himself or of other things which in their turn serve man. The whole chain of these referential relations is one-directional; their ultimate direction and final reference is the Being of Dasein itself. Thus even Dasein's discovery of ontic beings manifests its primary concern about its own Being. Dasein is worldly, because its existence, i.e. concern about its own Being, discloses to it such a phenomenon as "world." "World belongs to Dasein" because its disclosure is based on Dasein's existence and because the whole chain of referential relations connecting the beings in the world refers to Dasein. All worldly relations are concentric, with Dasein at the center. "World" is a characteristic of Dasein because it consists of relationships which are, ultimately, Dasein's relationship to itself. Dasein, the ontological being, the being whose mode of Being is to be concerned about its own Being, is (in Kant's language applied to Heidegger) "the condition of the possibility" of (the discoverability, i.e. of there being such a thing as) the world.

There is no man/world, man/nature, *res cogitans/res extensa* dualism in Heidegger. Man and world can never be separated or even discussed in separation, for "world stands precisely for men in their relations to all that is" (*G* 33), for man in the totality of his relationships. Totality, here, does not refer to the sum total of things in themselves invested with a substantial existence in an abstract theoretical universe; it expresses the unity of Dasein's world as a continuous whole of interconnected relationships and the fact that this is the only unit (indivisible individual) in *Being and Time*. Anything less—isolated beings—is a fragment, an abstraction deficient in meaning. It is true that Heidegger's "world as a whole" never embraces all the things in the world (in the traditional sense of the word). But all the abstract substantial entities thus neglected do not make Dasein's world any less complete: The "things" Dasein is not related to in any manner are not "at hand" (*pragmata, zuhanden*) and can thus never become "merely present" (*vorhanden*) to it and do not in any way belong to its world. Their substantial existence (in the traditional sense) in a hypothetical universe independent of Dasein can be neither asserted nor denied: "if there is no Dasein, then there is no 'independence' or 'in-itself' either. Such things are then neither comprehensible nor incomprehensible. Beings in the world are then neither discoverable nor can they lie in concealment. *Then* one cannot say either that beings are or that they are not, although one can say *now,* as long as there is an understanding of Being and thus an understanding of mere presence, that beings will still continue to be *then*" (*BT* 212/255. Heidegger's italics). There can well be a problem of "independent substantial existence" as long as Dasein exists. The very problem, however, is grounded in *our* understanding of Being and is thus dependent on that of which it must be independent in order to be "in itself" rather than "for us."

There is nothing particularly novel in this argument, nor is Heidegger's conception of the relativity of the world to human Dasein revolutionary. Heidegger is well aware of this fact, and in his essay *Of the Essence of the Ground* he cites a number of similar man-related notions of the world in the history of philosophy in support of his thesis. *Kosmos* in pre-Socratic philosophy, he argues, did not designate the things themselves but rather their mode of Being. *Kosmos houtos* did not differentiate one portion of what is from another portion, but it distinguished this world (one manner of Being) from another world (manner of Being) of the *same* beings. Heracleitus (fr. 89) related *kosmos* to fundamental modes of human existence, so that at the very beginning of Western thought "world" really stood for a manner of Being which was in some sense prior to all beings and was itself "relative to human Dasein" (*G* 22). Early Christian thought sharpened and reinforced this conception of the world to such an extent that in Paul and John "world" came to mean the mode of Being of Dasein itself, the quality of being human as such, in contrast to divinity, and Augustine and Aquinas used *mundus* as a name for humanity in general, for its particular state of Being, in which it is preoccupied with the world and oblivious of God (*G* 23–25).

Eighteenth-century German academic philosophy (e.g. Baumgarten) contrasted the world as the totality of finite beings with that which is not an *ens creatum,* and in his early writings even Kant accepted this definition. His great

merit was, however, that he defined the "finitude" of beings
in the world not so much in reference to their having been
created by God as in reference to their being known by
finite human knowledge. Thus the world became phenomenal, i.e. relative to our experience. In Kant, the world can
still be thought of as a totality, but "concepts of world"
(*Weltbegriffe*) refer only to "absolute totality in the synthesis of appearances" (*First Critique,* B 434) and not to the
absolute totality of the synthesis of the conditions of all
possible things in general. The latter concept—the transcendental Ideal—is quite different from the cosmological
Idea which is a transcendental concept of the totality of
the conditions of phenomena, an a priori representation of
an "unconditioned totality" which, transcending any and
all phenomena, refers back to them as objects of possible
experience. Thus in Kant "world" becomes a name for finite
human experience as a whole. It expresses, as Heidegger
puts it, "the totality of the finitude of human existence"
(*G* 31).

Without accepting all the connotations of the pre-Socratic, Scholastic, and Kantian concepts of the world, Heidegger claims to carry on this tradition. What is essential
in the early uses of *kosmos, mundus,* world, he argues, is
that they too "aim at the interpretation of human Dasein
in its relation to all that is" (*G* 33–34. Heidegger's italics).
As such they foreshadow his conception of the world as
the unitary whole of Dasein's relationships, and are the
historical background of his view that "world belongs to a
relational structure that is characteristic for Dasein as
such, the structure that has been named Being-in-the-
world" (*G* 34).

2. Having concluded his reflections on world and worldliness, Heidegger turns to the question concerning the being
whose mode of Being is to be-in-the-world. In view of the

analysis just completed it is evident that this question is directed toward Dasein. In the traditional language of philosophy we might say that Dasein is the subject of Being-in-the-world, provided, of course, that by "subject" we do not mean a substantial self or enduring identity of fixed qualities that is given in the world along with other substantial subjects and objects. Dasein is not a fixed substance actually given in experience, but a being that understands itself as its own possibility of being and becomes what it is by projecting itself into its self-disclosed possibilities. Its "givenness" has to be understood as self-disclosure, so that the question concerning the givenness of this subject means: in what manner does Dasein give, i.e. disclose, itself to itself in everyday existence?

Heidegger's answer is straightforward, as far as it goes. In everyday existence Dasein is not given, does not disclose itself to itself, as an authentic self, but as a self that is not truly its own, not the "I" that I am and which is mine, but merely a public image, as it were. As a rule, the subject of the phenomenon "Being-in-the-world" is the general "one" (the German *"man,"* indefinite pronoun, one like many). Everyday existence is dominated by the "others"; these others, however, are not particular individuals but the public in general. They might be anyone, and they are no one in particular. They are the embodiment of the public, the mysterious average person, the fictional common man, etc. In everyday existence *one* acts according to the way to act, *one* does not do what is not done, *one* is pleased, excited, outraged by whatever is commonly regarded as pleasing, exciting, outrageous, *one* follows laws, customs, public manners, and fads unthinkingly, *one* does simply what *one* is supposed to do. The subject of everyday Being-in-the-world is characterized by public conformity. This is a very seductive mode of existence, for inasmuch as the "one" dominates, decides, and seems to bear all responsibility, it seems to relieve every individual of its own decision and responsibility. Since everyday Dasein has a tendency to avoid these at all costs, it is almost irretrievably lost to the "one." Characterized by an utmost lack of personal independence, Dasein leads an unauthentic existence; "unauthentic" because its actions are never really its own.

3. The third structural moment of Being-in-the-world is Being-in (*In-sein*). Being-in is Heidegger's term for Dasein's self-disclosure as Being-in-the-world, in and by which disclosure the world and thus Dasein itself is "there" for, i.e. disclosed to, Dasein. The "there" (*Da*) in the name of *Da-sein* (being-there) names this essential disclosedness. One can speak ontologically of a *lumen naturale* in man, because, for Heidegger, Dasein, characterized by Being-in, is enlightened, is the light of its own existence as Being-in-the-world. "Dasein is its own disclosure" (*BT* 133/171).

The first ontological constituent of Being-in is "Finding" or "Finding oneself" (*Befindlichkeit*).[3] The term refers to Dasein's initial self-awareness, its awareness of the fact that it has been delivered into a world in which "it is left to itself" and "has to be" what it finds itself to be. This self-discovery of Dasein, "that it is and has to be," does not entail an explicit ontological understanding of the whys and wherefores of its being there. Finding itself, Dasein is merely brought face to face with itself and the "facticity" of its existence: that it has been thrown into, involved in, and

---

3. *Befinden* means to find, think, judge, deem, feel; *sich befinden:* to become aware, to notice; also, to be, to be found, in or at some place, to be well or ill; *es befindet sich:* it is the case, this is how things are; *Befinden* (noun): findings, opinion, also condition, state, circumstances; *befindlich:* to be found, situated; in existence; real; being. "Finding" and "finding oneself" are not exact translations of *Befindlichkeit* but they come as close to what Heidegger means as any single English word or phrase will.

committed to the mode of Being in which it finds itself, on its own, abandoned to its own limited powers and resources, without having any explanation of the fact (of its being-there) that is here revealed to it. Dasein may, of course, have or make up "rational" explanations for its existence, but such explanations are always subsequent to and grounded in its adumbrated disclosure of its facticity which is revealed to it in "finding itself" (*Befindlichkeit*).

To illustrate what he means, Heidegger gives fear as an example of Dasein's disclosure of its facticity. The phenomenon of fear discloses Dasein's Being-in-the-world and manifests its ontological nature in the following way: to be afraid means to apprehend something as frightening or threatening. But something can be frightening or threatening only to a being concerned about its own Being, and only within the system of referential relationships governed by this concern and established by Dasein's purposive, aim-directed disclosure of the world. Since the ultimate reference of all of Dasein's relationships is Dasein itself, whatever it may be directly afraid of or afraid for, ultimately it is afraid for its own Being. What is, therefore, disclosed to Dasein in this mode of "finding itself" that is called "fear" is not only its particular aim or purpose that the object of fear threatens, but, concomitantly with this discovery and implicit in it, the whole system of relations (the world) within which this object can be threatening, as well as its own nature as concerned about the possibilities of Being that it here discovers to be its own. In short, although the relational structure of Being-in-the-world is not explicitly, thematically disclosed in fear, fear is still a mode of Dasein's self-disclosure as an ontological being (concerned about its own Being), and of Dasein's finding itself as Being-in the world.

Another, more fundamental, mode of the disclosure of facticity is "dread." What distinguishes dread from fear is that while in fear one is, at least on the surface, afraid of and for something definite, dread is characterized by indefiniteness through and through. Not only is it impossible to point out any particular being as that which is dreaded, but the indefiniteness is of such degree that in dread all beings encountered in the world and all the particular concerns that make up Dasein's world become meaningless and irrelevant to Dasein. That which Dasein dreads is nothing and nowhere, for it is the world as such. The irrelevance of all beings within the world does not mean that in dread the world is in some way not there and that Dasein thus becomes unworldly. On the contrary, this irrelevance only discloses the world and its own worldliness all the more emphatically to Dasein: precisely because all beings are irrelevant, the world as such, i.e. as the realm of all purposive, referential, aim-directed relations, intentions, and concerns, becomes all the more imminent and oppressive. Thus, dread discloses Dasein as Being-in-the-world. Furthermore, the irrelevance of all beings isolates Dasein, and this isolation brings it to an inescapable awareness of its facticity: that it is and has to be what it is in the world. Dread is the most authentic mode of "finding oneself" in Heidegger, for it disrupts the everyday security of Dasein in the publicity of the "one," and, isolating Dasein, discloses to it its Being-in-the-world as that into which it has been thrown, as which it has to exist, and from which it has fled into unauthentic existence. In dread Dasein finds itself as an authentic self.

The second ontological constituent of Being-in is Understanding, a mode of disclosure just as original and fundamental as "finding oneself." Understanding is a technical term in Heidegger which has all the connotations of its conventional and philosophical usage, as well as some less usual ones. In German, the word *Verstehen* is used sometimes in the sense of *sich auf etwas verstehen, einer Sache vorstehen koennen, ihr gewachsen sein:* to be able to do something, to be capable of something, to be a match for something; and these connotations are included here. Understanding, in Heidegger, characterizes Dasein not only with respect to its intellectual faculties, but also with respect to its existential nature, i.e. as a possibility, potentiality, or power to be (*Sein-koennen*). The full meaning of understanding is: the self-disclosure of Dasein as a possibility, the self-projection of Dasein into its self-disclosed possibilities, and the projection, by Dasein, of the horizons which make all that is in the world possible and within which, therefore, all that is in the world can be (disclosed).

To see what this means we have to clarify Heidegger's unique notion of "possibility." Possibility, for Heidegger, is not a modal category of what is not yet but can possibly (i.e. not necessarily) become actual. Dasein's possibilities are its determinate nature or essence, provided that by "essence" we do not mean something altogether accomplished but rather something Dasein confronts as a demand it *has* to fulfill, i.e. something that is disclosed to it as its own "to-be," as that which it is and *has* to be. Thus its possibilities, far from conferring on an indeterminate Dasein a kind of negative freedom (*libertas indifferentiae*), are its self-disclosed necessities, the modes of Being into which it has been "thrown" and which it must now take upon itself as its own. They are not Dasein's essence, in the sense of an objective, impersonal, given nature, which it has whether it is conscious of it or not. Dasein's essence, its fundamental possibility—existence—is its own self-disclosure as and self-unfolding into what it has to be. (A rock does not "have to be" because it is not disclosed to itself and, therefore, it is not *faced* with any compulsion or demand but simply is what it is, while Dasein primarily "has to be".)

Heidegger's notion of possibility might be better understood by recalling that Dasein's "innermost" possibility in *Being and Time* is something that involves absolutely no choice of alternatives: death. Given man's biological constitution we would much sooner call death necessary than possible, but, for Heidegger, death is a possibility for Dasein because it is *revealed* to it as its own necessity, because Dasein is *related* to it as something that is its own inevitable end. Death is something Dasein "has to be," in the sense that by its disclosure death is taken up into the life of Dasein accompanying it as long as it lives. Death is not the actual moment at the end of life, but, by virtue of Dasein's relation to its own end, it is a "phenomenon of life." Dasein is "dying," facing death, as long as it lives and whatever its attitude toward its death—acknowledging, ignoring, enduring, or suppressing the thought of it; the fact that it takes an attitude indicates its awareness of its "extreme possibility," which, as the limit of all of Dasein's possibilities, points toward them and, by limiting them, defines them as a whole.[4]

Dasein's understanding of death determines Dasein's whole existence. By facing and enduring death as its own inevitable, inalienable, imminent possibility, of which it cannot be relieved, for no one but Dasein can die its own death, Dasein exists authentically. Since death claims not the public "one" but the individual self, since it is inevitably one's own, in the face of death Dasein is delivered unto itself, is exposed to itself in the nakedness of its existence. Unprotected by the distracting and comforting publicity of the "one," it stands alone reflected into the opposite of actual death, i.e. into life *as its own.* Understanding death as its extreme possibility limits Dasein's possibilities, and this limitation (this is all I am and have to be, by myself and now while I still am) makes them all the more urgent,

4. Concerning death as a possibility, see "Das Ding," in *Vortr* 177: "[men] are called mortals because they are able to die. To die means: to endure death as death. Only man dies. Animals pass away. They neither face nor ignore death as death."

pronounced, definite, and compelling, so that Dasein is all the more able to understand, i.e. face, accept, and endure, them authentically, as its own.

Dasein understands (its death and thus itself) because it is existential-ontological (related to and concerned for its own Being), and, in understanding, it understands itself as existential-ontological (related to and concerned for its own Being). Its understanding is at the same time based on, a manifestation of, and an insight into its existential nature. How completely this is the case in Heidegger we shall see in the following discussion of understanding not as self- but as world-disclosure, i.e. as Dasein's projection of the possibilities of all beings in its world.

Heidegger's notion of understanding as a "projection of possibilities" bears strong Kantian overtones and is, at least at first, reminiscent of Kant's conception of the role of understanding in human experience. In Kant, the a priori "conditions of the possibility of experience" do not belong to the things themselves but are our subjective contribution. We can know them, and the world as it is shaped by them, a priori, because we have contributed them in experience. Nature or the phenomenal world (the existence of things under a priori laws) can *be* because we contribute the conditions necessary for its existence. In Heidegger, understanding contributes, i.e. projects, the possibilities—modes of Being—of all beings in the world in a similar manner, and it is this projection of possibilities alone that makes the world possible. Possibility, here, means condition of possibility, that which makes something possible. Heidegger's possibilities, projected by Dasein in existence, are the ground—foundation and necessary form—of all that can be in the world, in the same way in which the Kantian conditions of the possibility of experience were the ground of all that could be objects of experience. Thus the projection of possibilities in "understanding" is an original mode of disclosure. It is this projection (of modes of Being, the conditions under which anything can be disclosed, i.e. can be a phenomenon, i.e. can be) that makes any disclosure (and Being in the sense of phenomenality) possible. Projection, here, has nothing to do with projects in the sense of a well thought out plan, nor does the projection of possibilities involve an explicit conceptual understanding of them on the part of the projector. As in Kant our contribution of the conditions of the possibility of experience did not hinge on the execution of a transcendental critique (the latter was merely an explicit, reflective, conceptual disclosure of the first), so now in Heidegger Dasein is already ontological—it factually projects the horizons within which anything can be—prior to and regardless of whether it ever engages in an explicit ontological analysis of its own structure, such as the one Heidegger undertakes in *Being and Time*.

When Heidegger speaks of Dasein's projection of "horizons" of possibility, he uses the word advisedly. *Horizon* in Greek means that which marks, bounds, limits, lays down, determines, defines. Since whatever is in no way determinate, definite, defined, limited, and finite, i.e. whatever has no characteristic mark, essence, or nature whatsoever, cannot be (phenomenal, i.e. visible, open to our sight), it is its *horizon* which gives a thing form and thus (phenomenal) being. It is in this sense that in both Kant and Heidegger man's understanding projects the horizons of the possibility, i.e. necessary modes of Being, of all that is (phenomenal/in the world). Horizon-projection is an image-making—the work of the understanding qua transcendental imagination in Kant—which gives form, brings to a fixed stand, lets something stand over against us as a definite something (literally, a *Gegen-stand*). It is the ground of all "objectivity," the ground of phenomena as well as phenomenality in Kant, and of world-disclosure, the disclosure of beings as well as the disclosure of Being-in-the-world, in Heidegger.

This great similarity between Kant's and Heidegger's views of world-projection should not disguise the fact that the difference between the two views is equally great. Their divergence becomes striking as soon as we reflect not on the fact of horizon-projecting but on the actual horizons projected by man in Kant and Heidegger. The problem of Kant's *Critique* was to account for a priori synthetic knowledge and thereby provide for the Newtonian natural sciences the firm foundation that they lacked in Hume. Heidegger's program is more far-reaching. He proposes to deal not only with man the knower but with man in all the aspects of his existence, all his modes of behavior and all his approaches to whatever he comes to deal with in his life. Therefore, while Kant's forms of intuitions and categories—projected in the Kantian horizon-making—are clearly defined, limited in number, easily exhibited in mathematics, and derived from the logical functions of judgment, Heidegger's "possibilities," projected by Dasein as the horizon of disclosure for all beings in its world, are wider in scope and unlimited in number, exhibited in everyday life, and derived from Dasein's concern for its own Being. They are neither as rigid nor as theoretical and neutral to practical life as the Kantian categories.

We have already seen this in our discussion of Dasein's worldliness, the first structural moment of Being-in-the-world. Dasein, the ontological being related to and essentially concerned about its own Being, approaches the world teleologically, discovers beings in terms of its own ends, and understands their Being in the referential context of its own concerns. In other words, the possibilities or modes of Being that Dasein projects for beings in its world are functions, related to each other by their "serviceability for" each other, and they are unified into one organic whole by their ultimate reference to Dasein "for the sake of which" (*umwillen*) and for whom they are what they are. A piece of chalk is not "an extended, relatively firm, whitish grey thing of a certain shape, and, in addition to all these, a thing to write with. The possibility of its being drawn along the blackboard and being worn away is nothing that we merely add to the thing as an afterthought. The thing itself, as this being, *is* in this possibility . . . In the same manner each being has in its own way such possibility inherent in it. This possibility belongs to the chalk. The chalk itself has a certain fitness to a certain use in itself" (*Einf* 23). And this fitness— or possibility—is the essence of the thing in Dasein's world. Dasein, concerned about its own Being, is essentially pro-spective, and its prospecting projects perspectives which open up a "region of relevant possibilities" (*N* 576). Exis-tential horizon-making and form-giving is always practical: it is ultimately directed toward making human existence possible.[5]

This being the case, it is easy to see why the particular forms, functions, or possibilities of Being that Dasein pro-jects in world-disclosure cannot be enumerated. They are as many as the practical aims of Dasein. It is equally obvious that things in the world, whose essence is what they are "good for" within Dasein's world, depend, for their essence, on Dasein's projection of their "possibilities." What a tree is—a thing to climb, to hide in, to grow, to cut down, to burn, or to investigate as to its biological, physical consti-tution—is determined by each particular man's relation to

5. Concerning horizon-making as a pro-spective projection of perspectives see also *Einf* 89; also Heidegger's discussion of Kant's Practical Reason in *N* I, 575–76. Although in his *Nietzsche* Heideg-ger deplores Kant's, and especially Nietzsche's, conception of the role of reason as practical, prospective-perspectival disclosure of the world in accordance with and in the service of the needs and demands of human life, what he says about their views applies to his own world-view in *Being and Time* at least as much as it does to Nietzsche's thought, and a great deal more than to Kant's.

it. Different modes of existence on the part of Dasein—whether it is as a child involved in play, a fugitive in search of refuge, a farmer, a forester, a merchant, or a scientist that man relates himself to the thing—open up different perspectives, project different modes of Being for the thing to be. The possibilities (modes of Being) of things projected by Dasein are relative to the possibilities (modes of Being) into which Dasein projects itself. As Dasein understands—discloses and acts out—its own Being, so it understands—discloses and acts toward—beings in its world.[6]

It can be objected to such a thoroughgoing humanization of the world that, representing a return to Greek teleology, it is an anachronism totally unsuited to be the basis of a modern scientific investigation of physical nature. But this objection has very little force against Heidegger's analysis of Dasein in *Being and Time*. For scientific investigation, with all its carefully worked out method and system of categories, is but one possible approach to the things in our world, and the role of the scientific investigator is but one possibility—mode of Being—among the many open to Dasein. It is certainly not *the* fundamental mode of Being in which Dasein always finds itself, and as such it is not the prime subject matter of a phenomenological description of human existence as such. And, since scientific investigation is not a fundamental mode of Being of Dasein, its method and its system of categories cannot be the framework within which to conduct an existentialistic analysis, because the method of the latter must be given with, indeed must *be,* the fundamental mode of behavior of Dasein as such. And this is Dasein's existence, i.e. ontological nature, concern for its own Being, on which the above interpretation has been

6. For a lucid discussion of this aspect of world-disclosure, see Anna T. Tymieniecka, *Phenomenology and Science in Contemporary European Thought* (New York, Farrar, Straus & Cudahy, 1962), p. 123.

based. Furthermore, the scientific approach is not only too limited to be the method and subject matter of an existentialistic analysis, but it is itself based on and characterized by Dasein's concern for its own existence. Scientific investigation, whether purely theoretical or practical-technological, is always motivated by some demand of human existence: the ontological demand, inherent in our (ontological) nature, to understand Being as such as well as our own Being in the midst of all that is, or the more direct and immediate demand for securing our existence by knowing, and thereby controlling, physical nature. The choice of the scientific method, with its impersonal, nonteleological, value-neutral categories, is governed by the above demands, and is thereby as teleological and aim-directed as the choice, on the part of the scientist, to engage in scientific inquiry. Therefore, science, as a human activity and a mode of approach by man to the world, can be and must be explained by way of an existentialistic analysis, while the reverse is not possible.

In view of the above, Heidegger has little reason to resent and try to refute charges of "humanism"[7] in what is, after all, an existentialistic analysis of *human Dasein,* while he can, with all justification, call the scientific approach a dehumanization of the world.[8] For reasons ultimately based on Dasein's concern for its own Being, scientific inquiry deliberately dehumanizes the world which, however, is first disclosed, and for the most part lived in, in an ontological, i.e. self-concerned and self-directed, manner. As such, sci-

7. Although, as we shall see, he both resents and tries to refute them in his later writings where he mounts his own attack against the "humanization of the world" by philosophers from Plato to Nietzsche. However, his objections to humanisms, as I shall try to show, are just as applicable to *Being and Time.*

8. He calls the process "de-worldlization," *Entweltlichung,* but, since "world" in Heidegger designates Dasein's world, the term is equivalent to dehumanization.

entific world-disclosure is but a derivative and privative mode of world-projection.

Before I can sum up my discussion of Heidegger's notion of Being-in-the-world, I must deal briefly with the third structural moment of Dasein's Being-in. This is what Heidegger calls Discourse. Discourse is a meaningful articulation of Being-in-the-world as disclosed in "finding" (oneself-in-the-world) and "understanding." Since without this articulation finding and understanding would remain altogether nebulous and vague, discourse is as original and essential a mode of disclosure as the other two. Discourse is expressed in language. As communication, which may take the form of speaking, listening, or being silent, Discourse manifests the existential openness of coexistent ontological beings toward each other.

In contrast with Discourse as a meaningful, articulated disclosure—to oneself and others—of Being-in-the-world, everyday talk (*Gerede*), with its high degree of ambiguity, is an unauthentic mode of disclosure. In talk, everything is understood because everyone moves on the same level of generality without trying to get to the foundations of what is being talked about. Communication is no longer a problem, since no one really attempts to appropriate what is communicated. Almost everything is self-evident and one cannot fail to understand anything, because understanding is not attempted but presupposed. In talk, understanding is more or less disrooted, it is a public good belonging to everyone and no one, and communication occurs on the ambiguous level of the everyday, public, generally known, common-sense "real world."

Talk, ambiguity, and curiosity—the urge to see, learn, and do, but not to appropriate—characterize Dasein's "fall" (*Verfallen, Verfallenheit*), a mode of Being in which, lost to and submerged in the publicity of the "one," Dasein's disclosure of Being-in-the-world is unauthentic in the extreme.

Dasein's "fall" does not, however, make it less of an ontological being, for it can only "fall" into a world which,
however unauthentically, it has itself disclosed, and it can
project itself unauthentically only into possibilities of its own
unauthentic projection. In other words Dasein can be alien-
ated from its essential selfhood, and it can be wrongly related to itself and the beings in the world, only because by
nature it is ontological: related to and concerned about its
own Being. It can disclose Being-in-the-world unauthentically, only because it is by nature the light, enlightenment,
and disclosure of Being-in-the-world.

Dasein's fall, although it does not make Dasein any less
ontological, does give rise to an "ontological problem": that
of the independent reality of the world. This "problem of
reality" comes as close to being a pseudo problem as anything could in Heidegger, for in view of the preceding existentialistic analysis it makes no sense for Dasein to raise
such questions as: "Is there a realm of Being that is transcendent to, i.e. independent of, human consciousness?,"
"Can the reality of this supposedly independent, external
world be proved?," "How can we gain access to this independent, real world and know it as it is in itself?" Inasmuch
as Dasein exists—and if it did not exist it could not raise
such questions—Dasein is always Being-in-the-world, and
the world is always given in, i.e. disclosed by, Dasein's
existence. Thus, raising these questions, Dasein questions its
own existence rather than that of some "independent reality," and an authentic insight into its own Being would
reveal this to Dasein, thereby preventing the emergence of
any "problem of reality." The persistence of this problem
is due only to Dasein's fall, this unauthentic mode of existence, in which the worldliness of Dasein is suppressed and
forgotten to such an extent that in the end it seems necessary
to Dasein to prove to itself the reality of the world. Since
Dasein exists for the most part unauthentically, it under-

stands and articulates its own Being—as well as that of all beings in the world—in terms of "mere presence" (*Vorhandenheit*), in terms of substantial, independent reality (literally "thingness") rather than genuine self-projected possibilities of Being, and it is this kind of understanding that leads to the "problem of reality." If all things in the world—ontological as well as ontic beings—subsist in themselves, regardless of their disclosure to and by Dasein, then their "reality," and that of our knowledge of them, becomes problematic. Since this is not the case, however, the problem of reality is merely the result of a "misunderstanding"—deficient mode of disclosure—on the part of Dasein. Even as such it manifests Dasein's ontological nature, i.e. that Dasein is characterized by an (authentic or unauthentic) understanding of Being. But the "problem of reality" can never be solved, even if unauthentic Dasein persists in raising it, because it is grounded in *our* understanding of Being, i.e. in that of which Being must be independent in order to be "in itself" rather than "for us." "If there is no Dasein there can be no independence or 'an sich' either" (*BT* 212/255).

Although Heidegger criticizes Kant for "trying to prove" the reality of the "external world" in his Refutation of Idealism, and sees the "scandal of philosophy" not in the fact that such proofs are unavailable, but in that they are expected and attempted, his criticism is altogether unjust. The main argument in both Heidegger and Kant is essentially the same: the interdependence of subject and external world in Kant, of Dasein and its world in Heidegger. Furthermore, Kant's discussion is as polemical as Heidegger's; it is a "refutation" of unjust claims and not an argument proffered as if Kant had thought it necessary to give a positive proof of the reality of a transcendent world within his transcendental critique. As we have seen (pp. 23–25), in both philosophers the world is a necessary projection of human understanding, coexistent with human understanding, and man's knowledge, or Dasein's understanding of Being, cannot transcend its own world-projection toward the knowledge of a transcendent reality.

In his essay *Of the Essence of the Ground* Heidegger repeats his argument for the interdependence of the self and its world in much the same terms as in *Being and Time,* i.e. in terms of the relativity of the world to human Dasein. The world belongs to Dasein because it is what it is—the totality of Dasein's referential relations—only with the existence of Dasein. Inasmuch as Dasein exists, the world "obtains" *(die Welt weltet),* and in the factual disclosure of the world Dasein is disclosed to itself as a being whose mode of Being is to be-in-the-world, related to and concerned with beings. Since all of Dasein's relations to beings other than itself are based on and are manifestations of its concern for its own Being, i.e. since the ultimate reference of Dasein's relations is Dasein itself, the disclosure of the world discloses Dasein itself (as this totality of relationships) and as a self (as a being concerned about its own Being). The interdependence of Dasein and its world remains the same: Dasein's concern about its Being is the presupposition—the ground of the possibility—of the world, while the world is a presupposition of the existence of Dasein as the being concerned about its own Being (since it is the disclosure of the world wherein the possibility of all concerns and relations, not excepting that of Dasein to its own Being, is grounded). Dasein and the world are neither independent nor related as one being (Dasein) to another (world), but refer to the same entity: Dasein as Being-in-the-world. As in *Being and Time* so in *Of the Essence of the Ground* Heidegger uses the word "world" in its original connotation: the age, time, era, i.e. life, of man, the immanent concerns of man, rather than a transcendent realm of independently subsisting things in themselves.

Disclosure as the Essence of Truth

I stated, at the beginning of my discussion of Heidegger's problem and method in *Being and Time,* that the problems of Being and of truth are closely related in Heidegger's philosophy. That this is the case is apparent as soon as Heidegger's conception of truth is presented. For even though truth has not once been mentioned by name, the existentialistic analysis of Dasein I have just completed deals with nothing but the phenomenon of truth in its various aspects.

Before making his conception of truth explicit—it has always been implicitly present—Heidegger reflects on the traditional concept and its ontological presuppositions. In his view, there are three theses characteristic of the traditional conception: "the locus of truth is the proposition (judgment)"; "the essence of truth lies in the correspondence between a judgment and its object"; and "Aristotle, the father of logic, is responsible both for relegating truth to judgment as its original locus and for initiating the definition of truth as correspondence" (*BT* 214/257).

Since Aristotle's statement, *pathemata tes psyches ton pragmaton homoiomata,* the definition of truth as *adaequatio intellectus et rei* has been dominant in Western philosophy. Aquinas, taking the definition from Avicenna, who in turn took it from Isaac Israeli's *Book of Definitions,* uses the terms *adaequatio, convenientia,* and *correspondentia* interchangeably, and in spite of all opposition to and departure from the ontological presuppositions of the definition, the definition itself has remained substantially unchanged up to the present time. To be sure, the concept of truth as *homoiosis, adaequatio,* etc. is quite general and empty. But, in spite of changes in the interpretation of knowledge, the concept has succeeded in persisting through all these years of human thought. To determine a reason for this, Heidegger analyzes the meaning and presuppositions of this relation of correspondence or adequacy.

All correspondence is a relation. This particular relation that is called truth is a relation between intellect and thing. But what are the presuppositions for such a relation? Does one have to understand the relation as one between subject and object in terms of a realistic epistemology, or can one clarify its meaning on the basis of human subjectivity itself? Truth belongs to the judgment, and in the judgment there is some kind of relation between a *real* physical fact, to which the judgment refers, and the *ideal* content of the judgment itself. Is this relation itself real or ideal or is it neither of these? And how can one grasp ontologically the relation between ideal being and physical entity?

Heidegger does not propose to answer these questions in terms of traditional epistemology or ontology. Instead of this he approaches the problem of *adaequatio* at another angle, designed to bring the phenomenon of truth more directly into focus:

When is the truth of a cognition evident? he asks. Obviously, when the cognition shows, manifests, or proves itself to be true, i.e. when it gives evidence of its truth. Cognition secures (makes certain of) its truth by manifesting, demonstrating itself. Take the proposition, "The painting on the wall behind us does not hang straight." The truth of this proposition shows itself if we turn to the wall and see the slanting picture. What is the meaning of this proof, what shows itself in the demonstration? Nothing if not that it is the thing on the wall that was meant, referred to, in the proposition. This shows that the whole complex of the judgment is a demonstration (monstration, exhibition, showing—not syllogistic proof) of "what is"; the judgment *discovers* that about which it is a judgment. What is shown in such demonstration is not a correspondence of cognition and its object, not a coming-together (*convenientia*) of something physical and something psychical, not an agreement between diverse contents of consciousness, but solely the discovery, the disclosedness of the being the judgment is about. It is the object itself that is shown as it is itself, i.e. as it is discovered and in the way it is discovered. In the discovery, the object shows itself qua itself, i.e. in its identity. The confirmation of the truth of a judgment is (based on) this self-manifestation of the object itself. Judgment and proof in cognition are themselves characterized by "being discovering," i.e. disclosing that which is as it is.

To say then, that a proposition is true means that the proposition discovers what is as it is; it pro-poses (puts forward, brings to light), manifests, shows that which is as it is discovered. The truth of a proposition, i.e. its "being true," must be understood as "being discovering" (*Wahrsein: entdeckendsein: BT* §44, especially pp. 217–18/260–61).

This definition of truth is, according to Heidegger, the *necessary* interpretation of what the oldest tradition of Greek philosophy had in some way felt and understood. The truth of *logos* as *apophansis* is *aletheuein* in the mode of *apophainesthai:* (to bring forth that which is, out of its hiddenness and to light, to let it appear, shine forth, in disclosure. In this sense, Aristotle, who grounded truth in the things themselves and identified *aletheia* with *pragma* and *phainomenon,* meant nothing else by *aletheia* (according to Heidegger) than the things themselves as disclosed. Heracleitus also had an insight into this nature of truth inasmuch as he understood *logos* as *phrazon hopos echei:* disclosing in what manner that which is is, i.e. disclosing that which remains hidden (*lanthanei*) to those who do not grasp the *logos.* Thus *a-letheia* (dis-closure) belonged to *logos* as *apophansis,* and the translation of *aletheia as* "truth" rather than disclosure only obscured what the Greeks had intuitively presupposed as self-evident in their use of the term *aletheia*.

To define truth as disclosure and not as correspondence is, therefore, not a break with tradition but the appropriation of the earliest tradition of Western thought. The definition is, furthermore, an organic result of the preceding existentialistic analysis of Dasein. This analysis of the different aspects of the disclosure of Being-in-the-world was, in fact, an analysis of the phenomenon of truth itself.

Being-true (*Wahrsein*) as being-discovering is a mode of Being of Dasein as Being-in-the-world. It is Dasein's purposive-prospecting circumspection that discovers beings in-the-world. These beings discovered by Dasein are true in a secondary sense, i.e. as being-discovered. All discovery of beings is grounded in Dasein's Being-in, i.e. in the disclosure of the world that happens necessarily with the existence of a Dasein that is the "there" (*Da*), the light and enlightenment of the world. The constituent moments of disclosure—"finding oneself," "understanding," and "discourse"—are at the same time the structural moments of truth. Inasmuch as Dasein is essentially characterized by disclosure, it is essentially "in the truth." Dasein's being-in-the-truth does not mean that it is ever initiated into or in possession of "all truth" (in the conventional sense of this expression); it means simply that disclosure belongs to the essence, i.e. existence, of Dasein. Heidegger elaborates on this in the following way:

Disclosure belongs to the Being of Dasein. As such it embraces the whole structure of its Being.

a. One of the constituent moments of this structure is "facticity," or Dasein's "finding itself" in the world. Disclosure is factual because Dasein always finds itself already disclosed to itself as a particular self delivered unto itself in a particular world in which it is related to particular beings.

b. Another moment of this structure is Dasein's existential projection of possibilities, or "understanding." Disclosure is characterized by existential projection, not only because Dasein's understanding projects the possibilities of Being of all beings it discovers in its world, but also because Dasein discloses itself to itself in terms of possibilities and projects itself into them, i.e. understands itself, authentically or unauthentically. Authentic self-disclosure or self-projection into one's own innermost possibilities is what Heidegger calls the "truth of existence." But existentiality, i.e. self-projection, belongs to disclosure even when unauthentic Dasein fails to own up to its own possibilities.

c. Discourse, the articulation of Dasein's "finding" and understanding itself in the world, is the third structural constituent of Being-in. As we have seen, discourse is for the most part an unauthentic articulation and communication, a mode of Being Heidegger terms "fall." Fall is characteristic of truth, too, for the most part. When Dasein discloses itself and the beings in its world in terms of public opinion, and lives in the climate of talk, ambiguity, and curiosity, accepting the generally accepted and therefore unappropriated "truths" uncritically, its disclosure distorts and hides authentic truth, the truth of existence. In the publicity of the "one," Dasein is in untruth. This does not mean that Dasein is no longer "true" (disclosing). On the contrary, it is because Dasein is in the truth (characterized by disclosure) that it can lose itself in unauthentic disclosure (understand and interpret its Being unauthentically) and thus hide authentic truth. Dasein's Being in the truth is not a static state of secure possession but a constant struggle to disclose authentically, on its own, to appropriate its own disclosure, to guard it from lapsing into forgetfulness and from being guaranteed not by the authenticity of disclosure but by the publicity of its acceptance. It is a struggle to strip uncritically accepted "truths" of their public sanction and

to test them in the light of authentic search, which alone can
result in authentic (self-appropriated) truth. Dasein is always in the untruth because it does not start with complete
ignorance, complete lack of disclosure, but with a disclosure
which is at best partial—thus hiding from Dasein its ultimate
concern—and at worst completely unauthentic. Thus truth
(disclosure) must be fought for. It is given only as untruth
(inadequate and unauthentic revelation) and must be wrested out of this concealment and brought to light in authentic
disclosure. It is this *steresis,* this wresting of something out
of its hiddenness (*letheia*) that the Greek alpha privative in
the word *a-letheia* expresses (see *BT* 219–22/262–65).

Granting for the moment that the original phenomenon
of truth is the disclosure of Dasein as Being-in-the-world,
it is not yet clear how this "original" conception of truth
could have degenerated into the "derivative" definition of
truth as correspondence, and why this derivative notion has
attained to such a dominant position in the history of
thought. Heidegger attempts to clarify this problem by
showing that the correspondence theory is but a modification of the original concept of truth as disclosure, and by
pointing out what it is in Dasein's mode of disclosure itself
that makes the derivative modification at first acceptable.

Dasein's aim-directed, prospective-purposive relations
to beings are a mode of discovery. What is discovered in
understanding is articulated in discourse and expressed in
language in the form of propositions. The propositions
communicate Dasein's disclosure, and a perceptive reception of this communication brings the receiver himself into
a relation of discovery with respect to the beings discovered.
The proposition, containing and preserving the disclosure
of what the proposition is about, makes this disclosure a
"piece of information," a useful thing, a utensil as it were,
which can be received and transmitted publicly. The receiv-
ers and further transmitters (of what by now is tra-dition)

are themselves still in a relation to the beings originally discovered, but this relation is no longer characterized by an appropriation and re-experiencing of the discovery. The disclosure contained in the proposition is objectified, it is regarded as a piece of factual information that is itself in some sort of relation to the object it is about, and when it comes to showing the truth of the proposition (originally: showing the proposition as discovering) this proof becomes a matter of showing its fitness, appropriateness, or adequacy to the object it refers to. This relation of adequacy (*adaequatio, correspondentia*) is conceived of as an objective relation between two objects (the information and the fact), and so the degeneration of the concept of truth from original disclosure to correspondence is completed.

The reason for this degeneration lies in the ontological constitution of Dasein itself: in the fact that in everyday life, in the publicity of the "one," Dasein understands its own Being in objective terms. Instead of discovering itself authentically as the being whose mode of Being is the disclosure of Being-in-the-world, it views itself as a subject (*hypokeimenon*) of such and such qualities, as a substance that is merely there (*vorhanden*) among other independent substantial objects. Within this "objective" interpretation, the derivative conception of truth as *adaequatio* is much more appropriate and plausible than the authentic understanding of truth as disclosure. Dasein, submerged in an "objective" world of everyday existence, remains in oblivion of the original meaning of truth, and the traditional concept, which is but an extreme derivative ontologically, becomes dominant.

"Truth, understood in its most original sense, belongs to the fundamental constitution of Dasein" (*BT* 226/269). The word truth names one of Dasein's *existentialia*. Truth, i.e. disclosure, is essentially a constitutive mode of Being of Dasein. There is no truth apart from or independent of

Dasein. " 'There is' truth only insofar and as long as Dasein
is" (226/269, Heidegger's italics). The laws of logic, the
laws of science, or any "truths" whatsoever are true only
insofar as Dasein exists. Before Dasein existed and after
Dasein is no more, there were not and will not be any
truths, because truth as disclosure was not and will not be
possible then. There can be no truths then because truth is
not something outside and above us to which among other
"values" we are related, but belongs to the Being of Dasein.
In order to maintain that there are eternal truths one would
have to prove that Dasein has always existed and will exist
forever. Lacking this proof, the assertion remains a "fan-
tastic claim."

All truth is essentially "relative to the Being of Dasein"
(BT 227/270). This does not make truth subjective in the
sense of arbitrary, for truth is an essential mode of Being
of Dasein, and precisely because this is so Dasein has no
arbitrary decision over it. Dasein cannot choose to disclose
or not disclose, because with Dasein existing truth factually
is and beings are disclosed as they are, i.e. as they reveal
themselves within the horizons of disclosure projected by
Dasein. Since Dasein has little choice with respect to these
horizons, since it does not freely create its own constitution
but is "thrown" into its modes of disclosure, the universality
of truths is assured, and truth is not in the least violated
just because it is relative to the human subject and happens
in and as the functioning of human subjectivity. (It was
precisely the subjectivity of knowledge and the phenomenality of experience that guaranteed universality and necessity in Kant.)

Why then must we presuppose that there is truth, and
what is the nature of this presupposition if truth is relative?
We presuppose truth simply because, existing as ontological
beings, we are in the truth. We do not presuppose truth
apart from or above us as an eternal value to which we are

related. Indeed, it is not even correct to say that we are doing the presupposing. Rather it is truth—disclosure—that enables us ontologically to presuppose anything. For what is the meaning of "presupposing"? It is "to understand something as the ground of Being of another being" (*BT* 228/270). But such an understanding of ontological relations is possible only on the ground of disclosure. To presuppose truth, then, means to understand it as the presupposition of the existence of Dasein, to understand it as that on the ground of which and for the sake of which Dasein exists. Dasein's mode of Being is to be concerned about its Being, and, since truth as disclosure belongs to the Being of Dasein, to presuppose truth really means for Dasein: to understand truth as its own ground, i.e. *to understand its own Being as disclosure.* We presuppose truth because with the existence of the "we" (Dasein) the presupposition is already, factually, made.

"We must presuppose truth" means that truth must be, since we exist. Truth belongs to the factual existence of Dasein. Dasein has never had and will never have a free choice as to whether or not it is to come into existence. In the same way it has no decision over truth. Independent of Dasein—*"an sich"*—it is not at all clear why beings should be discovered and truth should be; it is Dasein's factual existence alone that gives us ground for truth. Since truth is grounded in existence, or existence is grounded in truth— i.e. since Dasein's existence, the disclosure of Being-in-the-world, *is* truth—with the existence of Dasein, truth *is*.

The usual refutation of radical skepticism's assertion that there are no truths is not an argument of ontology. All it can show is that, inasmuch as judgments are made, truth is presupposed, but it does not reveal the ontological relation between truth and judging—i.e. that there is truth in judgments because judging itself is a mode of disclosure—and forgets the fact that even if no judgments are made there is truth (disclosure) inasmuch as Dasein exists. Radical skepticism cannot be refuted, because it cannot be proved that there is truth necessarily as long as the necessity of Dasein's existence is not proved. And this latter proof cannot possibly be given; Dasein can only presuppose its existence; it can never prove its necessity. A classical example of the impossibility of this proof is the Cartesian *cogito-sum*. Far from being a logical proof of existence— Descartes himself did not mean it to be that—the *cogito-sum* is the basic presupposition in Descartes' philosophy. It could never be proved because it could never be doubted, since such doubting would be self-refuting, because Dasein is not subject to proof with respect to itself. Descartes' *cogito-sum* was one form of the presupposition (of existence or truth) that had to be made because, with the existence of Dasein, it had already been made in fact. Fortunately, radical skepticism needs no refutation: it is self-refuting even in its most cogent argument for the nonexistence of truth or of Dasein. This argument—suicide—ends both existence and truth without proving, however, that there was none prior to the suicide. On the contrary, suicide points toward existence and truth, for, without existence and disclosure, suicide would not have been possible either.

"The Being of truth is originally conjoined with Dasein" (*BT* 230/272). And the same is true of the truth of Being. Only because Dasein is essentially constituted by disclosure can there be truth—i.e. disclosure—of Being. " 'There is' Being—not beings—only insofar as truth is. And truth *is* only insofar and as long as Dasein is. Being and truth 'are' equally originally" (ibid.) in every sense of the word. They are equally fundamental: they are the ground and source of all there is. They are (exist) equally necessarily, the one being as essential as the other. In the last analysis, they are the same. Being is truth.

Excursus

Before I go on with an exposition of Heidegger's philosophy, it might be appropriate here to make some observations
on what exactly the theory so far presented has to do with
what we ordinarily call theories of truth. It is true that
Heidegger is remarkably unconcerned with this matter; he
is even contemptuous of dealing with any practical application (in the ordinary sense of the word) of his thought, and is
opposed to entering any controversy about criteria of truth
and falsity. Nevertheless, any metaphysical theory, Heidegger's fundamental ontology not excepted, must have a
practical application in and for human knowledge, and must
yield usable criteria of judgment. Whether it does or not is a
test of its own truth (even in the Heideggerian sense of the
word). Heidegger's theory of truth, fortunately, satisfies both
these requirements. It gives a correct appraisal of the role of
disclosure in human experience, and, while it leads to no
new criteria of truth and results in no new principles of
applied judgment, it gives the traditional criteria a new, or
perhaps modified-traditional, foundation, justification, and
interpretation.

The simplest way to approach this problem of the application and criteria of Heidegger's theory is to ask ourselves,
What does truth as disclosure mean, and how does truth as
disclosure function, in our everyday experience? What is
error, and how do we distinguish in practice between truth
and falsity?

Truth as disclosure in everyday experience means, as we
have seen, the act and content of discovery, by Dasein to
Dasein, of beings qua beings. Concerned with its own Being,
bent on the purposes of its everyday existence, Dasein discloses beings (*as* good for, serviceable to, useless or even

harmful) in the context of its teleological, aim-directed
activity.

If truth in everyday experience is a disclosure of beings
qua beings, truth and Being are inseparably linked: each
new discovery enriches my world and enlarges my Dasein
as Being-in-the-world. Each disclosure of something as
something makes me aware of new modes of Being—of
myself as well as of the thing I am concerned with. In this
manner my whole world—the totality of my relations to
beings, and ultimately to myself—grows, and so do I myself
—as existent, i.e. self-disclosed Dasein. Dasein and its world
—the two are but one unitary whole—grow in meaning and
Being in the process of disclosure, the happening of truth.

Each truth—disclosure of something as something—is
particular, limited, relative, and subjective. What I discover
(the branches of this tree, e.g.) as a hiding place in one
particular situation (in flight or in play), I may discover as
a fruit-bearing, good-for-burning, -reaching, -throwing,
-building thing in others, depending on my particular concerns. And these concerns are equally particular modes of
Being and are discovered as such in the process of disclosure. Each new discovery limits and thereby widens the old
ones (this thing is not just a hiding place, it is also all these
other things), shows me their limits by transcending them,
and thereby expands the limits of my (and the things') Being
by its limited extent.

All discovery is inescapably relative and subjective, because what things I discover, and what I discover them as,
depends entirely on my particular modes of Being, i.e. the
possibilities I project myself into ("existentiality") and discover myself as thrown in ("finding oneself") in the disclosure. To the extent that my modes of discovery—existence
—differ from those of others, things will be (discovered as)
different to each of us, we will not live in "the same world,"
and communication will be possible only to the extent that

our worlds overlap. The fact that in everyday existence our subjective projects and concerns separate us to some extent is patent; exaggerate the difference and assume, for the sake of the argument, that our projects, approaches to and ways of life have nothing in common, and the "common world" disappears and communication becomes impossible. Both community and communication, the whole phenomenon of sharing truths, discoveries, i.e. "world," depends on our sharing (subjective) modes of existence, on our being alike. A perfect sharing, a perfect coincidence of worlds, the existence of universal truths only, would presuppose the perfect identity of all our modes of existence.

Scientific truths are objective (in the ordinary sense of the word) not because they are any less relative to the human subject's contribution; they are objective, i.e. shareable, i.e. intersubjective, because of our adoption, for the purposes of scientific disclosure, of a common project. In approaching the world scientifically, we deliberately eliminate all modes of approach which we do not happen to share or cannot share, we disregard the fact that we are particular individuals (musician, accountant, farmer, child) involved in the kind of activity particular to this or that mode of Being alone, and deliberately adopt a restricted mode of approach or point of view, through which alone we propose to approach and to view whatever we come in contact with. Thus the objectivity of scientific disclosure is guaranteed not by the supposedly objective nature of the thing itself—for this it has, theoretically, no matter how we approach it—but by our deliberately fixed subjective and, because agreed upon in advance, intersubjective, method (mode of approach, mode of Being). Science no more discloses the things themselves than does everyday experience. It does, however, prescribe in advance the nature of things (i.e. in what manner, as what alone, they can, and therefore have to, show themselves in the investigation) more narrowly

than everyday disclosure, with its great variety of particular
horizons, perspectives, and projects, ever will. The scientific
approach to the world is no less a projection, on our part,
of a world-view (what the world has to show itself as) than
is everyday disclosure. It is merely a more limited, impov-
erished, but therefore more shareable and intersubjective,
projection than that of everyday experience—rich and
varied but therefore not always shared or shareable.

We may, of course, assume that the world—of things in
themselves—was in some manner always there prior to our
disclosing it, ready to be discovered in all the diverse ways
we are capable of. We do, in fact, assume this whenever we
talk about our ways of disclosure as subjective and of the
world as phenomenal, i.e. my, our world, in the Kantian or
Heideggerian sense. But the proof and justification of this
theory is precisely our subjective and intersubjective disclosure of beings, which disclosure the theory itself is designed to explain and justify in the first place. The assump-
tion of the "independent reality" of the world has no meaning except in reference to the dependent, relative, subjective-
intersubjective phenomenal reality that anything has in *our*
existence. And this reality (i.e. thingness), governed by our
subjective or intersubjective existential projects, potentialities of disclosure, i.e. modes of Being, is the only reality for
us. That is what makes phenomenological theories of truth
(*aletheia: phainesthai: einai*), be they the Kantian or Heideggerian variety, eminently practical. Recognizing the relativity, subjectivity, or phenomenality of the world, the
inseparable unity of subjectivity and objectivity, they allow
us to concentrate on this world of our concern and bar all
speculation about the nature of what by definition can never
enter into and be part of our world, and is thus of absolutely
no concern to us.

Now if truth in Heidegger is this relative, subjective disclosure by Dasein of limited, particular modes of Being (of

things and of ourselves), untruth must be a similarly subjective and relative concealment or covering up of certain
modes of Being, and truth and untruth qua disclosure and
concealment must arise simultaneously. Since each particular disclosure is only partial and limited, each discovery
reveals and conceals at the same time: when I concentrate
—as I always do in practice—on the aspect of the thing
that concerns me in view of my particular concerns at the
time, this concentration itself obscures, at the time, most
other aspects—possible modes of Being—of the thing and
of myself, and leaves them unrevealed. Potentially these
so far undiscovered aspects are equally real or true: not in
terms of what the thing may or may not be in itself, irrespec-
tive of my disclosure, but in terms of my other potentialities
of disclosure which are as yet actually untrue, i.e. undiscovered and obscured precisely by my present exercise of
one particular potentiality of disclosure. What is actually
untrue—undisclosed modes of Being of myself and my
world—is therefore untrue in terms of my later discoveries
which, disclosing new modes of Being, make these true, part
of my world, part of myself, and thereby disclose the untruth
—partial truth—of the old disclosures.

Nothing in the world is ever absolutely true or untrue,
and everything is true and untrue at the same time, because
there are only limited, partial, relative truths and untruths,
made (partially) true and untrue precisely by their limits.
The fuel merchant viewing the forest only as a source of
firewood certainly discloses it to an extent—as does the
child, the scientist, the painter, the forester; but each of
these disclosures is limited and to that extent not fully true,
not fully disclosing.

Such disclosure becomes an error or untruth in the ordinary sense of the word when its limits are undisclosed and
its limited nature is left out of account. When a man believes
his limited disclosure to extend further and disclose more

than it actually does, he errs. His truth becomes untrue (in the ordinary sense of the word) because, and to the extent that, he fails to be aware of its limits, i.e. of his own as yet undisclosed possibilities of disclosure which will in due time limit, and thereby disclose in a new light, his present ones. Error is actual not because a man knows nothing—in this case of total lack of disclosure there could be no error or untruth either—but because he does not know enough and ignores the limits of his knowledge. Error or untruth (in the ordinary sense of the word) consists, in Heidegger as in Plato and Descartes, simply of holding a partial insight to be full disclosure. Thus untruth arises out of disclosure (that ignores its own limits) and is corrected by further disclosure (of the limits of the former disclosure). It is not (total) darkness but (limited) light that obscures; in Heidegger, as in Plato, it is "apparent" (i.e. partial but taken for full) disclosure that prevents further disclosure. Until further discovery shows an earlier one to be actually obscure and limited, the search for disclosure is interrupted in the particular area in question. It is only our projecting ourselves into hitherto unused possibilities of disclosure, modes of Being, that opens up new areas of Being and enlarges our world.

The happening of truth, the self-disclosure of Dasein as Being-in-the-world, is a never-ending process in Heidegger. It can end only with the end of Dasein qua Dasein: the being whose essence—existence—is to disclose. Since all particular disclosures are limited, since truth and untruth—disclosure and concealment—inevitably occur together, there is always more (world) to disclose, more (Being-in-the-world) to open up, more (Dasein, existence) to be. Final limits (of disclosure, existence, Being) are never reached, Dasein is constant growth: a growing beyond its own limits of disclosure and Being, a process of dialectic self-transcendence. Characterizing human existence as a process of self-

and world-disclosure, Heidegger's theory of truth in *Being and Time* not only yields us a clear description of the actual process of discovery in everyday empirical existence, it also yields us meaningful and usable criteria for acquiring and testing truth.

Empirical experience is a series of disclosures. We learn and grow when new discoveries throw light on the limits of the old ones, show them to be only partially revealing, and, therefore, in the light of the new discovery, to have been concealing, untrue. It is in this manner that experience is self-corrective and self-enlarging. If so, the measure of truth, as well as its criterion, is nothing but disclosure: the truth of any insight, opinion, or statement is directly proportionate to (the extent of) the area it discloses.

Traditional criteria of truth are in no way invalidated here; they are merely given a new and unitary basis in disclosure. Heidegger's criterion of truth might be called "correspondence," if by correspondence one means the correspondence of one disclosure to another rather than that of knowledge to independently existing thing. For the more disclosures "correspond," the more they unify experience and disclose it as a unitary system of referential relations. When "truths" overlap—concern the same area of referential relations—without corresponding, their overlapping (of disharmonious, nonmeshing lines of cross-reference) obscures and confuses rather than discloses and clarifies the focal area. Therefore lack of "correspondence" is lack of truth.

This is to say that one of Heidegger's criteria of truth as disclosure is simply "coherence." The incoherence or conflict of disclosures results in lack of disclosure. As Dasein's world is a unitary system of referentially connected relations, discoveries must be internally coherent or else they obscure, shadow, and hide rather than reveal (the referential structure of Dasein's world). Incoherence of disclosures prevents the clarification (disclosure) of Being-in-the-world as a unitary structure and is thereby an obstacle to truth, the enrichment and enlargement of Dasein's existence.

By the same token Heidegger's theory supports all the pragmatic-utilitarian criteria of truth, for criteria like workability, fruitfulness, guidance, simplicity, and economy are derivable from and justifiable in terms of truth as disclosure. The truthfulness of a hypothesis is directly proportionate to its extensiveness, i.e. the extent it either directly discloses or allows us to disclose. The leading or guiding function of a theory means nothing but a leading into or guidance in other and further areas of disclosure. Since Dasein's world has a referential structure—relations are ultimately connected by Dasein's concern—it must always be possible to move within it from one particular disclosure to another. Whatever disclosure interrupts this transition breaks the references and connections and thus conceals part of my possible existence and prevents the disclosure of my world. As for utility and workability, the only thing that makes a hypothesis more useful or workable than another is that it discloses more. Economy and simplicity are also a function of the extensiveness of disclosure. The simplest, most economical, fruitful, useful, and workable theory is the one that discloses most.

Heidegger's theory of truth not only reinforces the traditional criteria, but, with its insistence on the limited nature of each discovery and its emphasis on constant (self-) transcendence toward a larger and larger whole, it has in fact a great deal in common with many a traditional theory. In Plato too, opinion—true or false—consisted of partial disclosure unaware of its limits, rather than of total lack of disclosure; learning was impelled by the disclosure of the limits of previous disclosures; and the process of learning, which was at the same time the process of becoming essential, was a gradual ascent from fragmentary, disconnected,

confused, and obscure experience to more and more coherent, overarching and unified disclosure. And Hegel's
notions of untruth as limited, partial consciousness of self
and world, of Spirit as the restless drive toward self-disclosure, and of Truth as the Whole toward which all dialectic
is directed, are also clearly reflected in the Heideggerian
theory.[9]

One significant difference must, however, be stressed.
Heidegger, unlike Hegel and perhaps unlike Plato, holds
out no promise of absolute knowledge to man, in *Being and
Time*. Since vision depends on horizons, since everything
that is disclosed must be disclosed within limits that make
it visible by giving it form and shape, since all disclosure
is conditional—made possible by the particular conditions
of possibility of Being projected by Dasein's projecting itself
into particular possibilities of Being—finite disclosure is
ever-widening, but absolute truth, disclosure, and Being
are by definition impossible for Dasein to attain.

9. For a comparison of Hegel's and Heidegger's theories of truth
see Alphonse de Waelhens, *Phénoménologie et Vérité* (Paris, Presses
Universitaires, 1953), to which I am indebted here.

2.

HUMANISM, SUBJECTIVISM, NIHILISM

The theory of truth Heidegger expounds in *Being and Time* is so Dasein-related, man-bound, and relativistic that one would expect Heidegger to have a certain amount of sympathy for other theories, ancient and modern, that also emphasize the centrality of the human subject and its ways of approaching, disclosing, and viewing the world. It is surprising, therefore, to read a number of essays and lectures, written or delivered within a decade or so of the publication of *Being and Time*[1] in which Heidegger takes strong excep-

1. The exact chronology of *Platons Lehre von der Wahrheit,* "Die Zeit des Weltbildes," *Einfuehrung in die Metaphysik, Der Satz vom Grund, Die Frage nach dem Ding, Kants These ueber das Sein,* and *Nietzsche* is somewhat obscure. "Die Zeit des Weltbildes," which seems to be the earliest of these works—Heidegger still regards Descartes and not Plato as the initiator of humanism here— was first published in *Holzwege* in 1950 and, according to Heidegger, first delivered as a lecture in 1938. The Plato lecture, in which Heidegger considers Plato a humanist and regards the whole of Western metaphysics as humanistic, was written in 1940, published in 1942, but, according to Heidegger, delivered as a lecture as early

tion to what he considers to be humanistic, subjectivistic, and relativistic theories of truth. In "Die Zeit des Welt-bildes" he accuses Descartes of perverting the Greek notion of truth and thereby initiating the modern era in which man functions as the center of the universe and the arbiter of all truth. In *Platons Lehre von der Wahrheit* it is Plato who is taken to task for forsaking the original Greek concept of *aletheia* and initiating, with his theory of ideas, the hu-manization of truth that Heidegger deplores. Finally, in this essay as well as in his *Introduction to Metaphysics* and *Nietzsche,* the whole of Western metaphysics, from Plato to Nietzsche, is criticized for being humanistic and nihilistic and persisting in an "oblivion" of truth and Being.

This is a strange state of affairs. For how is it possible for Heidegger to engage in a polemic against "humanisms" when his own theory of truth is avowedly subjectivistic and relativistic to the extent that not only truth but even Being as such become relative to finite human existence? " 'There is' Being . . . only insofar as there is truth. And truth is only insofar and as long as Dasein is" (*BT* 230/272). Have we misinterpreted *Being and Time* or has Heidegger's theory

---

as 1930–31. The *Introduction to Metaphysics,* which more or less agrees with the Plato lecture on the humanist point, was published in 1953 but first delivered, according to Heidegger, in 1935. Kant is not accused of humanism in any book published before 1957, but at least one of the works (*Die Frage nach dem Ding*), in which such charges appear, was first delivered in a series of lectures in 1935–36. *Nietzsche*—which for the most part expresses the humanist charge but at times resembles "Die Zeit des Weltbildes" in exempting Plato from it—was published in 1961 but consists by and large of lectures delivered in 1936–40. The only safe conclusion to be drawn is that all these works (with the exception of those portions of *Der Satz vom Grund* which have no bearing on the subject of this Chapter) belong to the decade 1930–40 and express Heidegger's point of view during that period, especially during the latter half.

of truth, and with that his whole thought, itself undergone such a profound transformation in the years following the publication of *Being and Time* that it would allow him to view his own philosophy as nonhumanistic, and accuse others of humanism? The following account of Heidegger's discussion of what he calls three "decisive stages of the humanization of truth" will enable us to answer this question.

Plato's Theory of Truth

The aim of his work on Plato is not to repeat what Plato said explicitly, but to show what he "really wanted to say" and reveal the "hidden meaning" of his words. In accordance with this aim, Heidegger begins the essay with the following analysis of the cave metaphor in the *Republic* (514A–517A).

The cave metaphor is an illustration of the process of education (*paideia*). This process consists of a series of dynamic transitions from one stage to another. The transitions may represent either an ascent out of the cave or a descent back into it. What is common to both ascent and descent is that in each case the eyes are confused and have to go through a slow and painful period of adjustment until they grow accustomed to the light—or twilight—of the new situation and can thus discern whatever is visible in that light. A man, led out of the cave of his hardly noticed ignorance, is blinded by a more essential vision. But a return from these heights of essential knowledge into the dim depths of vulgar reality is no less perplexing. Each transition requires a profound transformation of the soul. This inner transformation is what Plato calls education. It is a *periagoge holes tes psyches,* a turning around of the whole soul, a leading of man out of his customary dwelling place and into another abode.

The cave metaphor's relevance for Plato's theory of truth is not evident, Heidegger argues, as long as we are content to translate *paideia* simply as education and *aletheia* directly as truth, especially if by the latter we mean *adaequatio rei et intellectus*. Correctly understood *paideia* is a transition of man from one abode to another and a corresponding conversion of the soul from what had been apparent to it before to what is now revealed. Transition and conversion are marked by a change in that which is disclosed, and in the manner of disclosure at each stage. But disclosure is *aletheia* in Greek, and so transition and disclosure, *paideia* and *aletheia,* are essentially related.

What Plato means by that which is disclosed (*alethes*), Heidegger continues, is whatever is present, apparent, and open to sight in a given situation. Regional truths (*alethes*) are relative; they are whatever is revealed within a given realm of disclosure. The truths of the cave dwellers are the shadows, those of the released prisoners the actual objects in the cave. Although the latter are truer, more disclosed (*alethestera*) than the former, they are still relative to the situation, and are but pale reflections of the truths of the third stage, the forms visible in the light of day. Disclosure at this last stage is the original truth. It impels, motivates, and gives direction to the whole process of education. "The essence of 'education' is (thus) grounded in the essence of 'truth' " (*PLW* 30).

Since *paideia* is nothing but a process of transition, an overcoming of hiddenness and a discerning of what is revealed in the situation, the metaphor does not end with the stage where man, delivered from the *apaideusia* of the cave, rests in the possession of the highest truth. There is a fourth stage: the dangerous descent. The liberated cave dweller returns to deliver those who remained below. Still blinded by the sunlight, he fails to make out what is disclosed (true) in the cave, and so the prisoners and their deliverer do not recognize the same truths. Once more the truths given in the situation—in this case the shadows—have to be appropriated, and an initial confusion accompanies the return just as it did the transitions of the ascent. Education, the "transition to truth," is always a privation. This is what the Greek privative (*a-letheia*) expresses. New truths must be wrested from (*a*) their relative concealment (*letheia*) and the new vision gained deprives us of our former sight. This process of privative attainment to disclosure is the essence of *paideia* and *aletheia*. And *aletheia,* disclosure as a transition from *apaideusia* to *paideia,* is what the Greeks meant by truth.

Although it is clear that in Plato the fourth stage of the cave metaphor had a bearing on the education of the cave dwellers who remained below rather than on that of the returned prisoner, this is not the place to defend Plato against Heidegger's attempt to "make explicit" what Plato left unsaid.[2] What Heidegger's interpretation best illustrates is, typically, his own theory of truth, and that is what concerns us here. So far, this theory is much the same in the Plato essay as it was in *Being and Time.*

In *Being and Time,* one of the ontological constituents of Dasein as Being-in-the-world is called Being-in. Being-in means that man, at any stage, be it in the cave or outside, always finds himself (thrown) in (to) a realm of truths (*alethes*) and is confronted with beings already disclosed in his particular area of disclosure. Insofar as Dasein exists, truth is factual, and the world is "there," i.e. is revealed. *Paideia* and *apaideusia* are necessarily related as truth and untruth, and Dasein is characterized by both, since truth, instead of being a static vision, is primarily an act, an existential possibility Dasein unfolds, and a constant struggle

2. For such a defense see G. Krueger, "Martin Heidegger und der Humanismus," *Theologische Rundschau,* n.f. *18* (1950), 148–78.

to overcome concealment and attain disclosure. This is why for Heidegger the return of the prisoner into the cave is just as much a transition to truth as was each stage of his ascent: the regional truths of the cave dwellers which he cannot immediately see must be disclosed to and appropriated by him. Since any transition to truth requires an effort and a painful transformation of the soul, it is understandable that man in everyday life—Plato's cave—is reluctant to give up his regional truths—the shadows—given in the public domain, and prefers to remain in *apaideusia, letheia:* unauthentic existence in the publicity of the "one."

Heidegger's discussion of Plato becomes more interesting for us at the point where he tries to indicate the differences between the original Greek notion of truth qua disclosure and the one he takes Plato's to be. For here his objections to Plato place his own theory of truth in a new and rather perplexing light.

In his account of *paideia,* Heidegger admits, Plato no doubt deals with that which is disclosed as well as with its manner of disclosure. But this treatment of truth, he charges, is only instrumental to something else: disclosure is important only because it lays the appearance (*eidos*) of what appears, the form (*idea*) of what is seen, open to sight. What matters to Plato is not disclosure itself, but the appearance of the forms in the light of disclosure. The essence of a form is to "shine forth" and "be visible"; this makes truth—now the disclosure of the idea, the visible form— relative to the sight of the knower. Truth in Plato thus degenerates into a characteristic of the relation of sight and form, the knower and the knowable, and the ground of this relationship is something other than truth: it is the idea of the Good. "For this, that provides the disclosure of what is known and gives the knower the power (to know), is . . . the idea of the Good" (*Republic* 508A).

It is a grave misunderstanding, Heidegger continues, to

translate Plato's *agathon* simply as "the Good," and to invest this Good with moral connotations which make it a value, be it even the highest of values. In Greek *to agathon* means "that which is good for [fit, appropriate, suitable] and makes good for [empowers, makes fit, etc.] something" (*PLW* 38). The forms of Plato enable beings (*phainomena*) to appear, to show themselves (*phainesthai*) as what they are. As such they are the essence of beings (phenomena). The idea of ideas, the Good, is that which makes all sight, appearance, visibility, and disclosure at all possible. It is *tou ontos to phanotaton,* the clearest, brightest, and most apparent of all beings. Since the essence of all is the idea—the visible form—the idea of ideas, which makes all sight and visibility possible, is that which "enables par excellence," that which makes all possible: it is the ground of the possibility of Being of all that is.

By making the idea of the Good the ground of all disclosure Plato subordinated, according to Heidegger, truth to the idea (*he idea tou agathou . . . kuria aletheian kai noun paraschomene, Republic* 517C) and thus weakened the original character of truth. With the *idea* dominant over *aletheia,* the important factor in all our relations to beings is the right vision of the form (the *idein* of the *idea),* and man, in order to attain to truth, must be concerned, above all, with the correctness of his vision. This correctness (*orthotes*) is guaranteed if all sight is directed firmly toward the idea, because, thus directed, sight becomes "like," "fit," i.e. adequate to what is to be seen. Adequacy of *idein* to *idea* ensures *homoiosis,* a correspondence between knowledge and its object. With the predominance of *idein* and *idea* over *aletheia,* the foreground—the visible, thinkable form—rather than the essence—disclosure—of beings is emphasized, and truth becomes *orthotes,* correctness of perception and judgment guaranteeing a *homoiosis,* a correspondence of intellect and thing.

Heidegger deplores this change in the essence of truth—from disclosure to visible form, correctness of perception, and adequacy of judgment—because he regards it as a "humanization" of truth. While truth as disclosure has been an "original trait of beings themselves," truth as correctness of perception and judgment becomes a characteristic of human attitudes and relationships to beings. To interpret truth in this manner means to make man the criterion of all truth and Being. And this is what Plato does. Instead of concentrating on the essence of truth—disclosure—he lays all emphasis on a consequence, a result of disclosure: the idea, the visible, thinkable form. He takes an attribute—that something appears to our sight and thought—to be the essence of truth—disclosure of Being. This is a great mistake. For while it is true that *idea* necessarily belongs to *idein* and *noein,* it does not follow from this that our *idein* and *noein* are the decisive and essential measure of Being. To make them, and thereby man, the measure of all, is "humanism" and "subjectivism" pure and simple (see also *Einf* 137–41).

Plato's transformation of the essence of truth, Heidegger maintains, transformed philosophy. Truth having become a characteristic of the attitude and relation of the knower to the known, philosophy became a humanism: a restless circling around man in the attempt to secure his position in the midst of all. Even though man was not expressly elevated to the highest of all beings—since *paideia* was still directed to the last cause and ground of all Being, *to agathon to theion*—man's entire effort was expended on the correctness of his vision which, once secured, would secure his position in the world. Under the yoke of the idea, truth became relative to human sight, perception, thought, and discourse; it was understood in reference to "reason," "spirit," "thought," or some kind of "subjectivity"; and the original meaning of truth as disclosure of Being was forgotten.

This shift of emphasis from *aletheia* to *idea* was all the more fateful to philosophy as it affected the whole of Western metaphysics. Aristotle was no less "humanistic" than Plato. He, too, located truth in the understanding rather than in the things themselves (*ou gar esti to pseudos kai to alethes en tois pragmasin . . . all' en dianoia, Metaphysics* E, 4, 1027b, 25 ff.). So did Thomas Aquinas (*veritas proprie invenitur in intellectu humano vel divino, Quest. de veritate* qu. I. art. 4, resp.) and Descartes (*veritatem proprie vel falsitatem non nisi in solo intellectu esse posse, Regulae* VIII Opp. X, 396). Hegel's conception of absolute reality as Idea represented a highpoint in this process of humanization. And Nietzsche, whom Heidegger calls "the most unbridled Platonist in the history of Western metaphysics" (*PLW* 37), merely radicalized the process in pronouncing truth "the kind of error without which a certain kind of living being could not live. What is ultimately decisive is [its] value for life" (*Wille zur Macht,* no. 493).

The Cartesian World-View

Another decisive stage in the "humanization of truth" is, for Heidegger, Descartes' philosophy. In *Being and Time* Heidegger was already critical of Cartesian ontology. In *Holzwege* (in the essay entitled "The Time of World-views") and in *Nietzsche* (pp. 141–93) his polemic against Cartesian "subjectivism" becomes even more explicit.

With the liberation of man from subservience to the Church, he argues, man became the measure of all things in Cartesian philosophy. As the self-certain subject he is now the *fundamentum inconcussum veritatis:* an autonomous lawgiver who legislates truth and prescribes to the world in what manner and on what conditions it can be an object of human cognition. His approach to the world no longer lets beings show themselves as what they are, but, prescribing the manner in which they can appear, violates their pristine innocence. This method of approach is an attack on the world, staged by man, the center of the universe and the arbiter of all truth.

It was medieval Christianity that prepared the ground for the Cartesian view of the world, Heidegger continues. For Scholastic philosophy regarded as the essence of worldly beings their "having been created," and made a sharp distinction between faith on the one hand and knowledge and thought on the other. "Having been created" implied "having been preconceived," rationally thought of, having been an idea in God's mind prior to the actual creation, and, so, as soon as the bonds between man and his Creator began to be less binding, rational thought was hit upon as the natural substitute to faith, the latter an approach to the world that was now discarded. Delivered from the authority of the Church and deprived of the certainty of all truths he had up to then accepted on that authority, man had to find a new certainty, a certainty that needed no guarantee other than the authority of man's own mind. Descartes' *cogito-sum* fulfilled that requirement, and thus this new truth, the self-certainty of the subject, became the foundation on which all other truths could be based, the point of departure from which all other truths could be discovered with certainty. Man obtained a preferential position and became the measure of all things. Truth became relative to the clear and distinct perception of the self-certain subject. Though not a matter of individual caprice—for whatever clear and distinct perception might secure was binding for all men—it fell within the jurisdiction of man as a measure.

With this reorientation of man and change in the essence of truth, man's relationship to the world also changed: the *cogitatio* of the subject was no longer a humble, passive reception (*noein*) of the disclosure of what discloses itself, but it was a *co-agitatio:* a relentless grasping and securing of all by means of subjective criteria. In Descartes "man sets himself up as the measure of all criteria which measure and gauge (calculate) what can qualify as certain, i.e. as true, i.e. as real" (*Holzw* 101–02). This is an attack on the world. The subjectivity of man legislates the objectivity of all beings (i.e. in what manner and on what conditions they can be objects).

Since the self-certain subject wants to be certain of its world, and since the prototype of all certainty is the one known in mathematics, mathematical-physical calculation is chosen by Descartes as the method of approach. Within this method only that can be (an object) which satisfies the criteria, and so the method itself legislates the mode of Being of all objects. It is a project that designs the world on the basis of preconceived criteria. What is important in this approach is not that it operates with numbers and measurable quantities, but that it is "mathematical" in the sense that it constructs the world systematically within the horizons of *mathemata*. *Ta mathemata* in Greek designate that which is known in advance. Contributed by the subject, the *mathemata* of a system prescribe a priori the mode of Being of all that can be (within that system). It is of little importance whether the horizons thus projected are Platonic *idein* and *idea,* Aristotelian *theorein* and *ousia,* Cartesian *cogitatio* and *extensio,* Kantian experience with its forms of intuition and concepts of understanding, or even modern scientific method with its axioms and categories. In each case they are a systematic world-project: "Whatever aspect of a thing becomes amenable through them, constitutes the Being of that thing. In this manner, on the basis of a definite idea of Being, . . . Being is imposed on the 'world' " (*BT* 96/128).

This is the result of the Cartesian—or Platonic—change in the essence of truth. Where truth becomes subjective, i.e. relative to the human subject as the measure, philosophy becomes humanistic, i.e. primarily concerned with the subjectivity of the human subject. The world is no longer disclosed as it is on its own, but it is designed and projected on the basis of an interpretation of the "humanity," i.e. essence, of man. Like Plato, "Descartes does not allow beings in the world to manifest their mode of Being on their own, but, by means of an idea of being . . . which is of undisclosed origin and undemonstrated justification, he prescribes to the world what it can 'really' be" (*BT* 96/129).

The Kantian Critique

Descartes' humanistic, subjectivistic, "mathematical" approach to the world received an even sharper formulation, according to Heidegger, in the Kantian critique, which continued the Cartesian project of legislating the mode of Being of all objects on the basis of the subjectivity of the subject, and brought anthropocentric thought to a new height.[3]

---

3. According to his own account Heidegger has regarded the whole of Western metaphysics humanistic and subjectivistic as early as 1930–31. It seemed, therefore, bewildering to a reader who had followed his development that he singled out Plato and Descartes frequently for his attacks on subjectivism but consistently forbore to criticize Kant, against whom the same charges could have been made with at least as much cogency. This omission has now been rectified in a series of writings Heidegger published between 1957 and 1962 (*Der Satz vom Grund*, 1957; *Die Frage nach dem Ding*, 1962; *Kants These ueber das Sein*, 1962). As at least one of these works was conceived by Heidegger in the middle thirties (*FD* was, according to Heidegger, first delivered as a lecture course in 1935–36), and since the argument in all of them moves along the same lines as Heidegger's criticism of Plato and Descartes, I shall deal with Kant's "subjectivism" at this point, regardless of the later publication and uncertain chronology of these works.

Heidegger's reason for considering the critiques a new example of mathematical thinking are not far to seek. As it was not just Descartes' concern for mathematics that made his method mathematical for Heidegger, so it is not just Kant's justification of the use of a priori judgments in mathematics that makes him subject to the same charge. *Ta mathemata,* as it is once again explained in *The Question of the Thing,* designate whatever can be taught or learned about something. But teaching, in the strictest sense, is nothing but giving the learner what he already has, and learning, at its best and most difficult, means "to take real and profound cognizance of what we already know (*FD* 56). Thus we come to know things "mathematically" when we learn about them only what we can know about them in advance (*FD* 57). "Mathematical" is the disclosure of things "within which we always already move, and in accordance with which we can at all experience them as things and as such and such things. The mathematical is that basic attitude to things in which we represent things to ourselves only as what they are already given, and must and shall be given, to us" (*FD* 58). Mathematical knowledge is, therefore, knowledge of the a priori, a "knowledge about the fundamental presuppositions of all knowledge" (*FD* 58), a knowledge that "lays its own foundations and grasps its limits in the process" (*FD* 58). Thought is "thoroughly mathematical only when it thinks (about) itself" (*FD* 80).

By this definition, of course, Kant's critique, thinking of thought, establishing the foundations of thinking, and grasping the limits of thought, is a prime example of a mathematical philosophy, and, as such, it is open to the criticisms Heidegger leveled against Descartes. When thought turns mathematical, Heidegger charges, the self, the thinking subject, becomes not only the sole subject of thought but also *the* subject of all that can be thought; it becomes the ultimate ground (*hypokeimenon* in the literal sense of the word) of all beings (qua objects for the subject), the foundation on which all that can be (object for the subject) rests. Consequently Being degenerates into objectivity (for and in relation to the thinking subject), and subjectivity is established as the ground of all Being, certainty, and truth (*FD* 82). According to Heidegger, this is precisely what happens in Kant's thought.

In his most important works, Kant carried out a critique of pure (theoretical and practical) reason. But, Heidegger asks, what does "critique" mean? A critique is a rational inquiry that aims at clarifying the structure, determining the scope, ascertaining the power, and making safe the use of what is inquired into. Therefore, when a critique is turned upon reason itself, its aim is "the self-knowledge of reason confronted with and left to itself. Critique is thus the execution of the innermost rationality of reason" (*FD* 96); it is self-directed thought whose sole dimension is "the I-ness of the I; the subjectivity of the subject" (*SG* 132). In this dimension, of course, objectivity can have no other basis than subjectivity.

Kant's critique of pure reason is a critique of "the faculty of fundamental principles" (*SG* 131), Heidegger continues. But "faculty" (*Vermoegen*) means power, the ground in which something originates, and "fundamental" is whatever underlies something as its ground. Thus a critique of pure reason as the faculty of fundamental principles is a critique of reason as the "founding foundation," the "ground-laying ground" (*SG* 131) of all. In Kant's critique, pure reason, the pure subjectivity of the subject, becomes the "ground-laying ground" of the conditions of possibility of all objectivity (of experience as well as of objects of experience). "Critique of pure reason means a demarcation, on the basis of our reason, of the determinations of the Being of beings, of the thingness of things; it means an admeasuring and projecting of those fundamental principles of pure reason on whose basis a thing is determined in its thingness" (*FD* 95). As a mathematical inquiry, the critique provides a sufficient ground "for objects as objects of the self-certain representing subject" (*SG* 132), and thus establishes reason, i.e. human subjectivity, as the measure of "what can and what cannot appear as a being to man, and in what manner that which appears can appear and in what manner it cannot" (*SG* 131). Kant's thought is self-grounding thought in a double sense: it takes its own measure, finds its own foundations and grasps its own ground, and, at the same time, it lays itself down as the measure and ground of all. This is what makes it a continuation and radicalization of the Cartesian project in Heidegger's eyes.

Kant calls his critique transcendental philosophy, and transcendental it is for Heidegger too, but this does not make it any less mathematical-subjectivistic: "The critical delimitation of the objectivity of objects does (indeed) transcend all objects. This going beyond objects is, however, nothing but an entering into the realm of ground-laying fundamental principles, into the subjectivity of reason" (*SG* 133). Thus the transcendental method is in effect thoroughly immanent: it remains completely within the region of the human subjectivity that it investigates. This immanence of the investigation results in the immanence of the subjectivity of the subject in the objectivity of any and all objects of human experience (*SG* 134).

"Objectivity of objects," Heidegger continues, is Kant's term for the Being of beings (*SG* 134), and that is why Being is no real predicate for him, i.e. that is why the proposition "a thing is or exists" adds nothing whatever, according to Kant, to the concept of the thing represented. In Kant such a proposition merely "posits" the thing in a certain relation—that of objectivity—to the representing subject. "Ob-jectivity" (*Gegen-staendigkeit*) and "ob-ject" (*Gegen-stand*) must be understood here literally as "standing over against the subject"; the words themselves connote a "relation to the thinking I-subject, from which relation Being obtains its meaning as 'position' " (*KTh* 22). Being qua position naturally does not say anything about *what* the object is, it says something only "about the *how* of the relation of the object to the subject" (*KTh* 24). Consequently Being and the modes of Being—possibility, actuality, necessity—cannot be derived from the (material content of the) object because their sole origin and foundation is human subjectivity (*KTh* 26). "All the objectivity of objects rests in subjectivity" (*SG* 137) here, and this inordinate emphasis on the subjectivity of the subject as the ground of Being (qua objectivity) makes Being altogether relative and subject-related in the Kantian critique.

Truth, the disclosure of Being, becomes equally subjective in Kant, for all truth—qua *objective* disclosure—is grounded in the highest principle of synthetic judgment (*FD* 143), and according to this principle the subjective conditions of the possibility of experience are at the same time the objective conditions of the possibility of objects of experience. Instead of revealing Being in an unconditioned way—by letting it reveal itself of itself as it is in itself—the Kantian approach to the world thus makes all revelation (i.e. truth) subject to the same subjective conditions which condition (*be-dingen*) all things (*Dinge*) qua things (objects). Our subjective constitution thereby becomes the Unconditioned, that which alone is neither a thing nor something conditioned, (*FD* 7): the unconditioned and absolute ground established by the Kantian critique as the ground on which all future metaphysics has to stand.

Kant's thought is, Heidegger concludes, a thoroughly anthropocentric project. More radically even than Descartes' attack on the world, it makes man the measure of all things. "Kant's inquiry into 'things' inquires into intuition and thought, it inquires into experience and its fundamental principles; this means: it investigates man. The question: What is a thing? is the question: Who is man?" (*FD* 188–89). The critique of pure reason is humanism pure and simple: a circling around man as the absolute foundation and perfectly sufficient ground of all truth and Being.

Nietzsche's Metaphysics

The last stage in the humanization of truth is represented by Nietzsche. In Heidegger's view, Nietzsche is not just a poet-philosopher in revolt against an all too rigid and lifeless tradition. He is, rather, an accomplished metaphysician with whose thought the whole of Western metaphysics is accomplished, i.e. completed and brought to an end.

There are two crucial elements in Nietzsche's thought, according to Heidegger: the "will to power" and the "eternal return of the same." In *Nietzsche* these two are interpreted "metaphysically" in the following manner.

Nietzsche conceives the Being of all that is as the will to power. "Will to power" means "willing one's own power" or "willing one's own will," and that is the same as "willing one's own Being." Willing one's own Being is not equivalent to a Darwinian will to self-preservation, if self-preservation implies keeping and maintaining what one already is. Rather, "every willing is a willing-to-be-more" (*N* I, 72), a will to self-affirmation in the sense of increasing, heightening and strengthening what one is essentially. The will to power is the self-creative drive common to all beings. It is a "willing to get away from one-self" (the self one already is), a willing to grow "beyond oneself" (the self as already accomplished) and a "willing to be oneself" (the self that has yet to become what it essentially is) (*N* I, 161). But this self-transcending, self-unfolding will is the essence of life itself, and so in Nietzsche the Being of all beings, the world as a whole, is nothing other than life. The essence of all that is, life, is the will to power, the will to Being. Since the Greeks, too, conceived of the world as a whole as living, animated, besouled, self-moving *physis,* Nietzsche's philosophy is a return to the origins of Western metaphysics.

Nietzsche's emphasis on the "eternal return of the same" does not introduce an additional, different, and, as it is sometimes regarded, contradictory doctrine into his metaphysics. On the contrary, Nietzsche conceives of "Being, i.e. the will to power, *as* eternal return" (*N* I, 28); "the will to power *is* as eternal return" (*N* I, 160) for him. He "thinks of Being as time" (*N* I, 28), and "will to power," "eternal return," Being, and time are, therefore, but so many different names for the ultimate metaphysical reality in his thought. "Eternity," the time of the return, indeed the return itself, can be understood in Nietzsche only on the basis of the moment, i.e. "that time in which future and past meet" (*N* I, 356) in human existence. Thus "the temporality of the time of *that* eternity which must be thought of in the notion of the eternal return of the same is the temporality in which above all and, so far as we know, alone man stands, insofar as he forms and endures the present while resolutely facing the future and preserving the past" (*N* I, 357).

Now all this sounds very much like a translation of Nietzsche into the language of *Being and Time,* and one might expect Heidegger to approve of the theory thus translated. But once again Heidegger detaches himself from what he describes and raises questions that implicitly charge Nietzsche with a "humanistic" perversion of "truth": does not such a man-based and man-bound notion of temporality, he asks, entail a humanization of the eternal return as well as of the will to power, and, thereby, of the whole of what is? Is not the conception of human temporality as the process of the unfolding of the will to power, the will to Being, the will to self-transcending life, an eminently "human" notion based on our insight into ourselves, rather than into Being? And does not this kind of insight inevitably lead to a humanization of Being as such? Can any philosophy that starts with such anthropomorphic terminology ever hope to escape being a "humanism," i.e. an anthropomorphic interpretation of the world as a whole? Finally, if Plato's and Descartes' philosophies were already subjectivistic and humanistic, what is the meaning of Nietzsche's so-called revolt against traditional metaphysics?

Heidegger answers these questions by contrasting Plato's and Descartes' "humanism" with the thought of Nietzsche in order to see whether Nietzsche's intended and well-publicized revolt against traditional philosophy ever came off. His finding is that what Nietzsche hoped to achieve and what he ultimately achieved are two entirely different things: Nietzsche interpreted Plato's theory of ideas "all too externally and superficially" (*N* I, 585) and therefore thought it necessary to oppose his own doctrines to Plato's notion of "preexistent ideas." But, due to his superficial understanding, this opposition resulted more in a translation of Plato's thought into a modern idiom (*N* I, 586) than in a true reversal of a trend.

For Nietzsche the most significant step in Plato's metaphysics was the division of all beings into two worlds of unequal ontological rank: the "true" world, the world of Being, the world of ideas or forms, on the one hand, and the "apparent" world, the world of Seeming, the world of phenomena, on the other. The first of these worlds, amenable to knowledge and containing all reality, was the repository of all truth and value, and the second, approached by means of the senses and lacking in reality, was a world of illusion and semblance. Truth, knowledge, *eidos,* and *idea* were thus clearly separated from and opposed to illusion, opinion, *eikona,* and *eidola.*

But what kind of reality is amenable to a knowledge of

preexistent "fixed" ideas, Nietzsche asked? A reality brought to a standstill, a changeless realm of universal essences. Consequently, Plato's emphasis on knowledge makes all truth and Being a matter of permanence, stability, and immutability. Now if Being is life, the will to power, the eternal return of the same in the moment, as it is to Nietzsche, Plato's metaphysics must be reversed and all stress must be laid on his second world, the world of becoming and movement. This results in a radical revaluation of knowledge. Knowledge does not become altogether worthless, but whatever value it retains must be derived from its value for life, the will to power, the will to Being.

"Knowledge . . . is, in essence, the schematization of a Chaos" (*N* I, 559), Heidegger interprets Nietzsche; "to know means: to impress ordering forms on Chaos" (*N* I, 562). Chaos is not sheer disorder and confusion; it is simply this world of "drive, flow and motion, whose order is hidden and whose law is not immediately known" (*N* I, 566). Chaos is "the hiddenness of the unmastered abundance of the becoming and flux of the world as a whole" (ibid.). What then is the value and truth-value of a knowledge that schematizes and brings to a standstill all reality? On the one hand, all truth inherent in such knowledge is nothing but illusion, distortion, and deception. On the other, however, this kind of illusion is necessary for life, this "truth is the kind of error without which a certain kind of living being could not live" (Nietzsche, *Wille zur Macht,* no. 493). Therefore knowledge as a "schematization of a Chaos in accordance with (our) practical needs" (*N* I, 559), as a form-giving governed by the perspectives of our existence, is simply a necessary condition of life itself. In order to live we have to know, but life is higher in value than knowledge, and knowledge, while it makes life possible, no longer leads to truth. Truth—disclosure of Being—is attained to not in knowledge but in art which, as a creative, self-transcending movement, is not so much about becoming and life as it is true becoming and life itself. "Art transfigures life and elevates it into higher, as yet unlived possibilities which are not 'over and above' life but rather reawaken life, out of itself, to a quickening wakefulness" (*N* I, 567–68). Art is therefore truer, or what is the same, of more worth than knowledge and its truth, and Plato's evaluation of the relative truth and worth of knowledge and art has been completely reversed.

Unfortunately, for Nietzsche, Heidegger regards the result of this Nietzschean inversion of Plato "in essence identical" with the theory inverted, and claims that a metaphysical position does not become any less metaphysical by being merely stood on its head. To be sure, Nietzsche was sharpsighted enough to see that Plato's "transcendent" ideas and values, to which human knowledge and conduct had to be subordinated, were in effect the outcome of man's work. He saw that with their creation man had "set himself up as the measure of the meaning and value of things" (*Wille zur Macht,* no. 12) and it was only a kind of "hyperbolic naïveté" that made man unconscious of this fact. This is why Nietzsche proposed to do away with this unconscious "hyperbolism" and declared all truths and values man-made and human life to be the ultimate source of all truth and value. But such a conscious and deliberate "hyperbolism," Heidegger argues, is no less hyperbolistic—in the sense of man "casting himself up and beyond himself" as the unconditional source and end of all—than Plato's, and an acknowledged humanism is no less humanistic than an unacknowledged one. It is merely the explicit fulfillment and radicalization of what was inherent in Plato and ever since Plato in the tradition of Western metaphysics: "Metaphysics is anthropomorphy—the shaping and viewing of the world in accordance with man's image" (*N* II, 127). In all metaphysics "man's relation to the whole of what is is decisive" (ibid.), because man has assumed "the role of being the unconditioned and sole measure of all things" (ibid.).

Although in Plato humanism was more implicit than explicit, Plato's metaphysics was just as much the result and expression of man's will to power as Nietzsche's. Nor was it any less nihilistic, for "metaphysics is qua metaphysics essentially nihilism" (*N* II, 343): it is a process in which implicitly (Plato) or explicitly (Nietzsche) man becomes the measure of all things, with the result that man himself, as well as his whole world, becomes measure-less, aim-less, worth-less and goal-less. Man's *experimentum medietatis*— attempt to make himself the unconditional ground and center of all—leaves man himself groundless and centerless. What alone could and therefore must provide the ground for all human existence—Being as such—is in oblivion, and, instead of thinking of Being, nihilistic, humanistic metaphysics only thinks of the world in the image and for the purposes of man.

This occurred in Descartes, too, where man displaced the Christian God and became the absolute subject and the unconditional ground of all. The Cartesian *cogitatio* turned into *co-agitatio:* per-ception in the sense of a grasping, capturing, and securing of everything for our use (*N* II, 156). Cartesian perception, no less than Nietzschean knowledge, was subordinated to man's will to power and served for the establishment of man's "absolute rule over the earth" (*N* II, 166). When man becomes the preeminent subject, everything in the world becomes object—i.e. subject to his aim-directed calculations—and truth becomes an ascertaining and securing and subjecting of all things to our might. Then man's "relation to beings is the mastering advance into world-conquest and world-rule" (*N* II, 171). The final result of humanistic-subjectivistic-nihilistic metaphysics qua world-projection for world-conquest is the rise of modern scientific technology: no longer a contemplation and harmonious cultivation of nature but a violent attack that forces all that is to reveal itself in the manner most serviceable to our insatiable will to power. Modern technology is but an extreme scientific application of the theory—Nietzsche's—that brought traditional metaphysics to its fulfillment and end.[4]

Being and Time *as Metaphysics*

Heidegger charges Western metaphysics with a perversion of the original conception of truth from *aletheia* to *pleonexia,* from a disclosure of Being to a tool of man's violent self-assertion and self-aggrandizement in the midst of all. Is his own theory of truth any less subjectivistic, humanistic, and nihilistic than the views he criticizes? Has *Being and Time* transcended the anthropomorphism that Heidegger rightly or wrongly ascribes to his predecessors? Is Heidegger's method of inquiry any less an "attack" on the world than Descartes'? Does Dasein's *aletheuein* lead to a more original disclosure of Being than Platonic *idein* or Aristotelian *theorein?* Are Being and truth any less relative in Heidegger than objectivity and truth were in Kant? Is Heidegger's philosophy of the world of Dasein as Being-in-the-world any less a man-centered philosophy of life than that of Nietzsche? I shall try to answer these questions by returning to *Being and Time* and reflecting on what happens in Heidegger's elaboration of the problem and method of his inquiry into Being.

To conduct his investigation properly, Heidegger adopts a method called phenomenology (*BT* § 7). This adoption,

4. Instances of Heidegger's polemic against technology are too numerous to be listed here. The reader may obtain a fair idea of their substance by referring to *Vortr:* "Die Frage nach der Technik," pp. 22–40, and "Wissenschaft und Besinnung," pp. 58–66.

he emphasizes, does not subject the investigation to a limited point of view and a preconceived project, for phenomenology rightly understood is neither a point of view nor a philosophical discipline. It is merely a method, a method that aims at "the disclosure of what reveals itself as it reveals itself by itself." Phenomenology, as its maxim implies, simply tries to get "at the things themselves."

Now this sounds harmless enough. It appears almost as if Heidegger succeeded in formulating what phenomenologists are sometimes accused of trying to find: a presuppositionless method. The trouble is, of course, that if all that phenomenology stands for is this intention to get at the things themselves in their pristine innocence, at the truth undistorted by false methods of approach, then all philosophy is phenomenological in intention and the name phenomenology is well-nigh meaningless. What philosophy worthy of the name does not seek the undistorted truth? The title phenomenology, expressing merely this intention, is so empty in its generality that it cannot even be restricted to being just another name for philosophy. Presumably all our investigations, philosophical, scientific, or other, seek the truth within their limited domain.

Furthermore, phenomenology so defined is not yet a method. A method of inquiry is a way of approach to what is being investigated. If this way of approach is to lead anywhere—and unless it does it is not a method—it must have a definite direction: it must contain directives laid down for the inquiry in advance of the inquiry. These directions—what the inquiry is aimed at, where it is to begin, and in what manner it is to be conducted—are the projected horizons of the investigation. They guide the inquiry by giving it focus and framework, i.e. by prescribing what is, and in what manner anything can be, an object of the inquiry. But this means that the directives of the method make the inquiry possible not by providing a free access to all so as to bring to light the pristine truth of the subject matter, but rather by barring from the investigation all that is alien to the preconceived project. In other words, all methodical inquiry is necessarily systematic—the unfolding of a project—and "mathematical" in the Heideggerian sense. It is the *mathemata,* what is laid down in advance, the projected horizons of an inquiry, which make it methodical; a presuppositionless, "unmathematical" method is a contradiction in terms.

If phenomenology is to be a method then, its definition must contain more than an expression of the vague intention to "get at the truth" about the "things themselves." It must indicate what kind of truth is to be sought, where and in what manner we are to seek it, and by what criteria we can recognize it if it is found. It must indicate what kind of things and what about these things we are concerned with, how we are to approach them so they can "show themselves," and by what criteria their essence (what they are in themselves) is recognizable. In other words, a workable definition of phenomenology as a method of inquiry must define, for the purposes of the inquiry, the meaning of truth and Being.

Heidegger's definition of phenomenology does indeed seem to do this. Phenomenology as "the disclosure of what discloses itself by itself," i.e. as the disclosure of Being, is, at the same time, Heidegger's definition of "original truth" (disclosure of Being), of ontology (disclosure of Being), and of Being itself (as its self-disclosure). But this coincidence of definitions does not in itself make anything clearer. For "Being" and "disclosure of Being" are, as Heidegger himself sees, such fundamental and overarching concepts that they give the inquiry no direction at all. Phenomenology as "disclosure of Being" fails to qualify as a method, a way of approach.

What saves Heidegger's inquiry from failure due to total

lack of direction is not that he chooses phenomenology as a method, but that his real decisions concerning method are made before the adoption of phenomenology. The latter, as he himself admits, is merely a consequence of the former; it is the unfolding of a project laid down in advance.

At the very beginning of *Being and Time,* immediately after announcing its aim, Heidegger attempts to lay down the directives for his investigation by way of elaborating the "formal structure of the inquiry into Being" (*BT* § 2). This attempt to specify (a) what is in question, (b) what is to be interrogated about that which is in question, and (c) within what conceptual framework the answer should be given, articulated, and regarded as acceptable, threatens to miscarry because of the fundamental nature of the problem. The problem of Being is so all-encompassing that the inquiry into Being is undirected by virtue of the overabundance of possible directions. Heidegger's solution of this difficulty is ingenious: declaring that man's inquiry into and understanding of Being makes him the prime subject of an ontological investigation, he decides to focus the inquiry not on Being as such—for this provides no focus—but on the mode of Being of that being whose nature is to inquire into and to understand Being. In order to do ontology (investigation of Being), he asserts, we must first engage in "fundamental ontology," an investigation of the ontological being (the being that already inquires into and has some comprehension of Being). Ontology must again begin as an existentialistic analysis of Dasein.

The importance of this step should not be underestimated, for Heidegger's decision to engage in fundamental ontology projects the horizons for the entire investigation that follows and turns *Being and Time* into a humanistic, subjectivistic, and relativistic philosophy.

A relativistic philosophy is characterized, according to Heidegger, by giving man a preferential position in the midst of all, by making him the measure of all that is, and by circling, incessantly, about man as the absolute center of all things. By this definition, *Being and Time* is relativistic. Fundamental ontology places man squarely in the center of the inquiry and interprets all things on the basis of man's attitude to and understanding of what he encounters.

A subjectivistic philosophy, according to Heidegger, is one that concentrates on the human subject and approaches the world on the basis of a preconceived notion of the subjectivity of man. By this definition, *Being and Time* is a good example of subjectivism. For having made man the point of departure for the investigation, it secures all truths from this point, and the whole investigation is but a systematic unfolding of the project laid down in advance. Since ontology has been turned into *fundamental* ontology, the method of inquiry becomes *hermeneutic* phenomenology: an interpretation, exposition, and clarification of man's understanding of Being. Since phenomenology is hermeneutic phenomenology, it is no longer "the disclosure of what discloses itself as it discloses itself by itself," but rather *Dasein's* disclosure of what *it* discloses in the way *it* is able to disclose. In other words, ontology has become philosophical anthropology, an analysis of transcendental subjectivity. It is by no means surprising that, after a long and laborious inquiry, even truth and Being turn out to be relative to human existence in *Being and Time*. This outcome was implicit in the project laid down at the beginning. An investigation that starts with man's disclosure of Being as its only guiding light is doomed to close with truth, the disclosure of Being, relative to and "happening" in human existence.

Such an investigation is nothing if not mathematical in the sense in which Heidegger uses the term in reference to Descartes and Kant. In *Being and Time* Heidegger makes Dasein, the being that reveals, not only its own exclusive subject of inquiry but also *the* subject, *hypokeimenon,* i.e.

the ultimate underlying ground, of all revelation and of all beings revealed. Characterized by a hermeneutic circle— being a disclosure of Dasein's modes of disclosure—*Being and Time* is self-grounding thought in the same sense in which the Kantian critique was: in it Dasein takes its own measure, understands its own possibilities and limits, grasps its own ground, and lays itself down as the measure and ground of all. Heidegger's mathematical inquiry, just like Kant's, transcends objects only to enter into the realm of a new subjectivity (Dasein's existence) and to circle within its dimension. Thus it remains as immanent (within human subjectivity) as the Kantian critique, and legislates all Being just as immanently (on the basis of this subjectivity). Kant's transcendental philosophy was, in Heidegger's words, "the execution of the innermost rationality of reason" (*FD* 96). Just such a radicalization of Dasein's existence is Heidegger's fundamental ontology. The critique tried to attain to "the self-knowledge of reason confronted with and left to itself" (*FD* 96). *Being and Time* aims at the same type of disclosure of Dasein's modes of disclosure. It has to, for mathematical philosophy—Descartes', Kant's, or Heidegger's—cannot accomplish anything else.

A humanistic philosophy, in Heidegger's eyes, constructs the world on the basis of a preconceived idea of man, so that in the course of its investigations it can confront nothing but its project, which it unfolds. By this definition *Being and Time* is nothing but a humanistic "attack on the world." It begins with a kind of Copernican revolution that puts man in the center (§ 2), it continues with the elaboration of a totally anthropocentric method (§ 7), it characterizes human Dasein as Being-in-the-world (§ 12–13), and on the basis of the structure of the modes of Being of Dasein it unfolds the world as the totality of Dasein's modes of Being (§ 12–24). Since Dasein is concerned about its own Being, the world becomes the complex of Dasein's concerns. Since

Dasein is directed toward its own Being as its own final purpose, the world becomes the totality of Dasein's purposive relationships (with Dasein at its center), and all that is in the world is encountered as a utensil located within a teleologically referential context. Since Dasein is the being that discloses, the world "happens" (*weltet*) in its disclosure (by Dasein), the mode of Being of beings in the world is their "being discovered" (by Dasein), truth is disclosure (by Dasein), and Being itself is relative to the existence of Dasein in which it is disclosed. This is a humanization of both truth and Being. Heidegger objects to Western metaphysics on the ground that in it truth is no longer located in the "things themselves" but in the human understanding. But in his philosophy the things themselves are, and are what they are, only in Dasein's disclosure of the world, so that here not only truth but even Being is located in the human understanding. The systematic unfolding of a preconceived structure can never arrive at anything other than what is presupposed in the project. It can only make explicit what was implicit in the presupposition. Since the basic presupposition of Heidegger's investigation in *Being and Time* is an interpretation of the essence of man, *Being and Time* cannot be anything but a "humanism."

In a brief passage (*BT* § 62) Heidegger himself admits that his existentialistic analysis has a preconceived idea of Dasein as its presupposition: "But is not the preceding ontological interpretation of the existence of Dasein based on a certain ontic notion of authentic existence, on a factual idea of Dasein? Indeed it is" (*BT* 310/358). Philosophy, he continues, should never deny its presuppositions, but should grasp them, understand them, and, unfolding them, it should unfold that which is based on them. But then, is this analysis as the unfolding of a preconceived project any less humanistic or any more legitimate than Descartes' "attack"? Heidegger thinks so, for he believes *his* project to be a necessary one: not an arbitrary plan conceived by the man Heidegger, but one prescribed by the very essence of Dasein. Since his presuppositions are not really presupposed by Heidegger the philosopher but are presupposed in and with the existence of Dasein, the project has a "positive necessity."

This argument, however, only complicates the problem. Heidegger's project does indeed have positive necessity if it is given with the existence of Dasein, and if it is the only possible approach, on the part of human beings, to Being as such. But this means that the humanization of truth is itself necessary and inescapable. Man qua man inevitably interprets Being and truth anthropomorphically and anthropocentrically, and Western metaphysics is engaged in an inquiry absolutely essential to man; it is, indeed, a "metaphysics that necessarily happens as Dasein" (*KP* 208). Metaphysics has to be humanistic, subjectivistic, and nihilistic, because man—the ontological, or as we might say now, metaphysical being—is what he is. This is, after all, what the unfolding of Heidegger's project in *Being and Time* seemed to prove. Therefore, either *Being and Time* is a well-conceived project whose unfolding only shows its positive necessity, and then all philosophy qua philosophy is humanism; or the possibility of a nonhumanistic philosophizing, of a direct rather than man-related disclosure of Being, remains open, and *Being and Time* and the whole of the existentialistic analysis of Dasein has to be abandoned as a way of approach to truth and Being.

It is this second alternative that Heidegger adopts, at first implicitly and then more and more explicitly. Although he still argues at times that a subjectivistic interpretation of *Being and Time* is a misinterpretation, he admits that the work was all too open to such an interpretation. The fact that he sees himself compelled to go on reinterpreting *Being and Time* in a vein that departs more and more from an existentialistic analysis of Dasein also witnesses his growing conviction of the inadequacy of his earlier method. He soon voices this conviction in so many words: the project of writing the second half of *Being and Time* had to be abandoned because the method and language of *Being and Time* were too "metaphysical" and prevented him from making explicit what he had really tried to say (*Hum* 17). This does not mean that his problem has changed in any way, for the only problem animating his philosophy is the problem of Being or truth, i.e. the disclosure of Being. But fundamental ontology—the investigation of Being by way of an inquiry into Dasein's ontic understanding of Being—can no longer be considered the right way to do ontology proper. The "things themselves," as they reveal themselves in our everyday intuition and understanding of them, are too much the result of our own projection, and are too laden with the unanalyzed conceptual constructs of twenty-four hundred years of humanistic philosophy. In confronting them phenomenologically, we merely confront what we have put into them through all the history of Western thought. Owing to its humanistic starting point, the existentialistic analysis is therefore incapable of overcoming the oblivion of Being and humanization of truth that has plagued Western metaphysics since Plato.

What, then, can be done? Can we escape humanism and the concomitant oblivion of Being only by abandoning all "human" understanding of Being, and, if so, what other understanding is open to us? Furthermore, if we repudiate the whole of our philosophical heritage from Plato to our own time (if this is possible), are we not abandoning the only guiding light that is still left to us in our perplexity? Heidegger has a twofold answer to these questions.

In the first place, it is neither possible nor necessary to abandon human understanding in order to avoid humanism. It is not possible, for "all understanding of beings, and especially of the whole of what is, is as an *understanding* by man already related *to* man" (*N* I, 357). "All representation of the whole of what is, all interpretation of the world, is therefore inescapably humanization" (*N* I, 358). It is obvious to anyone who cares to think about the problem that "with all his representation, intuition and definition of what is, man is always driven into the impasse of his own humanity" (*N* I, 358), and thus humanization as such cannot be altogether avoided. What can be done, however, indeed, what must be done, prior to a final evaluation of the pros and cons of humanisms, is to raise the question "What is man?" once again, in all seriousness. To be sure, it is necessarily man that asks the question and thereby defines his own Being, but there is a whole world of difference in how, and on what basis, man does the defining. For "it is possible that the execution of the determination of the essence of man always and necessarily remains a task for man, and is insofar human. But it is no less possible that the determination itself, i.e. its truth, should elevate man beyond himself and thus *de*humanize him and thereby invest the *human* accomplishment of the determination of the nature of man with another (nonhuman) nature" (*N* I, 361). All that is necessary is that the question itself should overwhelm man anew with all its might, so that man can define his own essence on the basis of what overwhelms him and makes the question itself necessary: of Being as such, rather than of the Being of man. Instead of defining Being on the basis of a definition of human nature—as apparently all metaphysics, including *Being and Time* has done—we have to attempt to define man on the basis of a definition of Being.

This new program is, in a sense, an explicit reversal of the method of *Being and Time*. While the problem (of Being) remains the same, the methodical emphasis is shifted to where it should have been all along: to Being itself rather than man. Heidegger's turn (away from the method of *Being and Time*) is designed to turn our eyes (away from man) into a new, but really forever existent, direction: the direction of Being.

With this new direction of thought, however, a new method is needed. Phenomenological hermeneutic, as an investigation and description of the things themselves as they show themselves in Dasein's everyday world-disclosure, led to "nihilistic humanism" and had to be abandoned. But can we now find a new method if phenomenology, as explained in *Being and Time,* is but another name for ontology and is therefore *the* method of all inquiry into Being?

Heidegger solves this problem by simply reinterpreting the meaning of phenomenological hermeneutic: it is not really the case that phenomenology was the wrong method, but rather that the method of *Being and Time* did not deal with the right phenomena. In Dasein's everyday understanding of Being, Being did not manifest itself (*phainesthai*) unobstructed and undistorted. We have therefore to look for a more original manifestation. The opposites of Dasein's everyday feeling and doing are the uncommon experiences of artistic creation and ultimate human freedom. Perhaps in these extreme situations Being reveals itself more originally than anywhere else. The opposite of Dasein's immediate intuition and everyday understanding of Being is the exceptional, fundamental, and all too rare insight that is vouchsafed to a few great men in the history of human thought. Perhaps it is in the work of these men, the great philosophers of the past, that the true self-revelation of Being takes place. If so, they are the true subject matter of phenomenology, and we do not have to discard the whole tradition of Western philosophy to get on with our study; on the contrary, we have to understand this history more originally than it was ever understood. To avoid the oblivion of truth that past metaphysicians lived in and contributed to, we have to interpret their work more originally than even they understood them; we have to reveal the hidden meaning of their words. And this is, for the most part, the new method of Heidegger's philosophy: phenomenological hermeneutic as an interpretation of the way in which Being manifested itself in and through the history of human thought. Does the new method lead to fundamentally new results?

3.

TRUTH AND BEING

Truth and Freedom

The first essay[1] that attempts explicitly to abandon "every kind of anthropology and all the subjectivity of man as a subject" (*WW* 27) in order to effect "a change in the relation of thought to Being" (ibid.) is entitled *Of the Essence of Truth*. It begins with Heidegger's usual criticism of the traditional concept of truth, that the definition of truth as *adaequatio rei et intellectus* reduces truth to a matter of correctness, the correctness of the relation of knower to known. And, since any epistemic relation presupposes a region of disclosure within which region alone a relation to that which is disclosed is possible, the relation of disclosure precedes all other relations.

1. The exact chronology of the works I deal with in the following is still obscure. *Vom Wesen der Wahrheit* was first published in 1943, but it supposedly contains the revised text of a public lecture delivered repeatedly since 1930. (The second edition of this work differs from the first only by the addition of one paragraph to the "Conclusion"). *Holzwege* was first published in 1950, but different versions of "The Origin of the Work of Art" were delivered as lectures in

86

This argument is nothing new. We have encountered it in *Being and Time* and other early writings. What is novel in this essay is the introduction of a new concept in the definition of truth: "The essence of truth is freedom" (*WW* 12), Heidegger now proclaims. But what is freedom? Freedom means "to be free for the overtness of something overt" (ibid.), to be free for the disclosure of what is disclosed within the openness of a region of disclosure. That which is disclosed within this region are the beings man is related to insofar as he is free, i.e. open to disclosure. Man's freedom for the disclosure of what is disclosed "lets beings be," lets them be "what they are" (*WW* 14). Freedom as "letting beings be" is the opposite of leaving them alone; it implies a commitment and involvement with what is; it is an entrance into a realm (of disclosure) in which alone whatever is can be (disclosed, a phenomenon). In other words, freedom is an "ex-posure"—Dasein is ex-posed, it ex-sists, stands out—"into the disclosure of what is" (*WW* 15). It is Dasein's "ex-sistent in-sistence" which preserves the disclosure of beings. "The disclosure itself is preserved in the ex-sistent involvement, through which the openness of what is open, i.e. the 'there,' is what it is" (*WW* 15).

All this is but another way of saying what has already been said in *Being and Time,* namely that Dasein is characterized by existence (here: ex-sistence), i.e. that it is in the

---

1935–36, while "Anaximander's Sentence" was written in 1946. *Was heisst Denken?* was published in book form in 1954 and it contains the unrevised text of a lecture course given in 1951–52, with additional notes and explanations that are undated. *Vortraege und Aufsaetze,* 1954, consists of lectures delivered between 1943 and 1953. *Unterwegs zur Sprache,* 1959, is a collection of pieces written or delivered between 1950 and 1959. *Gelassenheit* was published in 1959, but it was written, according to Heidegger, in 1944–45. *Identitaet und Differenz* and *Der Satz vom Grunde* were both published in 1957.

truth. It is the being that discloses by being open toward
(free for) that which may show itself as a phenomenon
(*alethes,* that which is disclosed) to a being characterized
by being disclosing (ex-sistent, free). Ex-sistent Dasein lets
beings be by contributing their possibilities of Being; it
contributes these possibilities because it is characterized by
being disclosing and because the Being of beings is defined
as disclosedness. They could not be (phenomena, could not
show themselves) but for the ex-sistence of Dasein. Even
Heidegger's remark that the ex-sistence of man begins in
the historical moment when the first thinker ex-poses himself to the disclosure of what is, by raising the question
concerning the Being of beings, is nothing new. Existence
was defined at the very beginning of *Being and Time* as
"the mode of Being in which a being is concerned about
its Being." It is in this mode of Being that disclosure is first
experienced, that the world discloses itself, and neither disclosure nor the world would be without man's ex-perience
(ex-sistence, ex-posure into it). The history of man and the
history of the world are the same history: the process of the
happening of truth (disclosure), and this history happens,
i.e. Being is disclosed, insofar and as long as man, the
being concerned about Being, exists.

Viewed in this way, the introduction of a new term (freedom) for what we have already encountered under the
names of existence, Being-in-the-world, being in the truth,
and understanding of Being, etc., is more confusing than
enlightening, and it certainly does not support Heidegger's
polemic against humanistic, anthropomorphic conceptions
of truth. If the essence of truth is freedom, and if man alone
has freedom, then truth is utterly bound up with the existence of man.

All this is admitted by Heidegger, but not without an
important qualification. It is true, he says, that man alone
is free, but it would be mistaken to assert that man "has"

freedom. Man does not possess freedom as a characteristic, rather "freedom, as ex-sisting, disclosing Dasein, possesses man" (*WW* 16). Freedom is not a quality of man; it is the source of his existence. Man is not the ground of freedom, except in the sense that freedom "grants itself" to man and employs (possesses) him as the ground for the unfolding of the essence of truth, i.e. the disclosure of Being. But in this sense it is not man, the historical being, that makes history —the process of disclosure of Being—possible; freedom, "granting itself" to man and making man ex-sistent, i.e. historical, makes him (possible as) the ground of history. Thus the existence of man is still necessary for the disclosure of Being, but it is no longer a sufficient ground; the final authority does not rest with man, for *man is no longer on his own*. With the introduction of freedom as the essence of truth we have arrived where the self is after the eradication of despair in Kierkegaard: the self (Dasein in Heidegger) is grounded transparently in the Power (freedom in Heidegger) which constituted and posited it.[2] The despair that is overcome in Heidegger is the despair of self-certain man as the absolute ground, center, and guarantee of all truth. The attempt to make man the unshakable foundation of all is over, and man, grounded in freedom, has obtained a new—or, perhaps, perennially old—fundament. How firm this new ground is in Heidegger we have yet to see.

With this shift of emphasis in the definition of truth, the nature of untruth also changes. Since freedom, the essence of truth, is beyond the power of man—being the power that posited him—and truth is not ultimately based on man's immanent search, untruth also becomes something more fundamental than just the result of incorrect knowledge, human failure, and ignorance. In *Being and Time* untruth had been defined as lack of disclosure, or unauthentic dis-

---

2. Kierkegaard, *The Sickness unto Death,* ch. 1, passim.

closure, and thus concealment of that which is, and truth
and untruth had been conjoined, since the existential constitution of Dasein made Dasein the being that disclosed
and concealed at the same time. (Disclosing specific objects
within limited horizons, Dasein covered up the totality of
what is, while, in the disclosure of the totality, specific
objects became irrelevant and were concealed.) This view
is not now repudiated, but it obtains, along with Dasein, a
foundation deeper than just the existential constitution of
Dasein itself. Untruth is still concealment and hiddenness,
but it is not so much relative to Dasein as it is taken up
into the ground of Dasein's existence (freedom): it becomes
the original mystery (*Geheimnis*) that permeates all disclosure. Freedom as the essence of truth is itself the living
tension of truth and untruth, disclosure and mystery. It
grants itself as this tension—the tension of the steresis in
a-letheia—and as such it constitutes the existence of Dasein.
To say that Dasein is exposed by freedom into the "open
ground" of disclosure means that Dasein is placed within
the tension of truth-untruth as the field in which the tension
obtains. The "original ground" of the tension is, however,
primordial freedom.

With this displacement of truth-untruth (from the existence of Dasein to the ground of this existence: freedom)
Dasein's unauthentic disclosure is no longer called untruth;
it is merely error or, literally, erring (*Irre*). Characterized
by "fall," lost to the publicity of the "one," interpreting its
own being on the basis of the objectivity of objects, Dasein
is erring. And in this erring or unauthentic self-interpreta-
tion, not only truth as authentic disclosure but also original
truth-untruth—the tension of original disclosure and concealment—are long forgotten and concealed. That is why
truth degenerates to adequacy and correctness, and untruth
becomes falsity in the sense of inadequacy and incorrectness
of knowledge.

Truth and Art

This conception of truth becomes even more explicit in the collection of essays entitled *Holzwege*. The general theme of *Holzwege* is presented in the first essay, "The Origin of the Work of Art," and I shall focus on this piece and refer to the others only occasionally as the subject matter demands.

Heidegger begins his essay on the origin of the work of art with a reflection on the thingness of the thing, but he soon abandons this approach as unsatisfactory and turns to a consideration of the essence of utensils. Utensils, being man-made things, have an intermediate position between mere things and works of art, and so an investigation of their nature might give us more insight into the essence of the work of art.

The essence of a utensil lies in its usefulness. The thing has been made to serve some purpose. These shoes in the shop window are designed to protect one's feet and give sure footing; they are made for work, mountain-climbing, dancing, or running, etc. But can we get at the essence of a utensil by taking a glance at one on display? Or do we have to look at a pair of boots where they are on their own? On the field, perhaps, where they do not meet the eye, where they are inconspicuous, unobtrusive, and yet in their own, since they serve? How do we get at the essence of a utensil?

There is a painting of a pair of peasant's boots by Van Gogh. Totally undistinguished ones, the kind he often wore, the kind that might be worn anywhere where people work near the soil, in Delft, in the Borinage, in Arles, anywhere. We do not know where they come from; not even a clod of heavy earth adheres to these boots, nor is there anything around them to indicate where they belong. They merely stand there, unlocated in space, exposed. "A pair of peasant boots, nothing more. And yet:

"Out of the dark opening of the worn boots gapes the toil of laboring treads. The massive bulk of the boots is sluggish with the weight of slow steps along far-stretched, windbeaten, forever the same furrows. The dampness and satiation of the soil permeate the leather. The loneliness of the way home in the dusk clings to the sole. The boots echo the unuttered call of the earth, its silent giving of ripening grain, its unexplained self-refusal in the fallowness of wintry fields. Uncomplaining anxiety about the safety of bread, wordless joy over the last bare escape from need, tremor at the advent of birth, trembling in the face of oncoming death—this is what passes through these boots" (*Holzw* 22–23). All the strands of a peasant's life are gathered within them, woven into a fabric and exposed to sight. This is the world in which these boots belong; the world of this peasant in which they are what they are since they are in their own. And that is the essence of these boots: to belong here, to gather in themselves the whole world of this man, to be another invisible yet all the more significant and comprehensive bond between man and earth, to be, in some way, a whole.

We have found the essence of a utensil, not through considering an actual artifact in production, on display, or in use, but by looking at a painting by Van Gogh. That has spoken and revealed to us what these boots really are.

What has happened? What is at work in the work of art? Revelation, *aletheia,* truth. A work of art does not so much reveal what this or that individual thing is as it discloses to us the essential nature and structure of a whole world. The simpler, the purer, the more primordial and unadorned the work, the more immediately and inevitably it does so. "In its way, the work of art opens up the Being of what is" (*Holzw* 28). This opening up or disclosure is the happening of truth. The essence of the work of art is thus the unfolding of truth. "Art is truth at work" (*Holzw* 28).

According to Heidegger this theory of art is by no means revolutionary; it is merely the revival of the original Greek conception. For *techne* and *poiesis,* as Heidegger never tires of repeating,[3] do not really refer to the making or producing of a thing and to the knowledge or skill requisite for this production. What *poiesis* creates is disclosure. Original *poiesis* pro-duces, leads forward, brings to light what is hidden and does not immediately show itself (by itself, *phusei,* "naturally") without this act of production. What is made, wrought, created in art is not a thing but, above all, disclosure. True *poiesis* is *aletheuein.* The essence of *techne* or *poiesis* is *aletheia.*

This is what distinguishes modern production and technology from *poiesis* and *techne* as conceived by the Greeks. The former is directed toward producing the things we need in our daily life and emphasizes the knowledge necessary for such production. The latter works truth by directing our attention away from the all too familiar realm of everyday existence, relegating the concerns of our vulgar doing, knowing, and making to utter unimportance, and throwing open the realm of the unfamiliar and extraordinary. Delivering us from the yoke of custom and convention, art transports us into this new realm: that of essential truth, the disclosure of Being. Art gives no knowledge for or impetus toward controlling the things of the world we are so fatally involved with. Rather, "it changes our usual relationships to the world" (*Holzw* 54), arrests our everyday public existence, lifts us ecstatically out of our obliviousness to the essential, and makes us succumb to and dwell in the original disclosure of Being.

This alone accounts for the fact that art is characterized by beauty. For beauty is not a matter of pleasing some sort of special aesthetic sense. Aesthetics as a particular disci-

3. E.g., *Einf* 121–23, *Vortr* 19–21, *Ar* 47.

pline among others can never explain beauty. The Greeks
knew this and consequently identified the beautiful, the
good, the real, and the true. To be beautiful means—in
Greek as well as in German—to shine, gleam, and blaze
forth, to appear in the light, to be revealed in one's essential
nature, to be disclosed in one's true Being. Beauty is disclosure. This is why Being and beauty belong together. For
Being is that which is most disclosed, the ground of all
disclosure, disclosure itself as such. Beauty, Being, and
Truth are but so many names for the same thing: original
disclosure.[4]

Plato was right when he held that "it is beauty's fate alone
to be *ekphanestaton* (that which most shines forth) and
erasmiotaton (that which is most to be loved)" (*Phaedrus*
250D). For "as the beautiful lets Being light up, and is as
the beautiful the most attractive,[5] it transports man out of
and beyond himself to Being" (*N* I, 228); "it wrenches us
out of the oblivion of Being and gives us insight into Being"
(*N* I, 227). This is what happens in the erotic possession:
"As soon as man, in his view of Being, lets himself be bound
by Being itself, he is transported beyond himself, so that
he extends, as it were, between himself and Being, and is
beside himself. This being-enhanced-beyond-oneself and
being attracted by Being is *eros*" (*N* I, 226). The aim and
outcome of this erotic-artistic attraction to and by Being
is truth, the beauty, i.e. disclosure, of Being. "What truth
accomplishes in its own nature—the revelation of Being—
this and nothing other is accomplished by beauty, as, shining forth in the apparition, it transports us into the therein
appearing Being, i.e. into the revelation of Being, into the
truth" (*N* I, 230). Plato's mistake was that he emphasized
our cognitive approach to Being at the cost of the erotic-

4. See *Einf* 100–01.
5. *das Anziehendste*, attractive in the literal sense of that which
draws us to itself.

artistic possession inspired by Being itself. This emphasis led to the oblivion of truth and Being, for "only insofar as Being (itself) is able to unfold the 'erotic' power in relation to man, only so far is man able to think of Being itself and to overcome the oblivion of Being" (*N* I, 226).

Apart from this emphasis on Being rather than man's existence, Heidegger's theory of art (in *Holzw, Einf, N*) might so far be an appendix to *Being and Time*. Art, disclosing the world as the totality of the relations within which the object represented by the work of art *is*—i.e. is significant, meaningful, what it truly is—seems to be just another way in which the world as a whole is revealed. The confrontation with the work of art, arresting our commonplace existence and disclosing essential Being, seems to be just another way to authentic existence. Dread is another mode of such disclosure, and authentic resolve—Being-unto-death—but another. All modes are but ways of the original history, i.e. process of unfolding, of the world, and the world still seems to be the totality of Dasein's relations and to belong ultimately to Dasein. The anthropocentric character of the theory, however, diminishes and the emphasis on Being grows as Heidegger continues his analysis.

Since the work of art "belongs in the region opened up by it" (*Holzw* 30), it may have been a mistake to look at a painting that represents so man-bound and worldly a thing as a utensil, whose essence could not be understood without an explicit reference to man. So let us consider another work of art.

A building, a Greek temple, is not the image of something else; strictly speaking it is not an image at all. It represents, in the literal sense of the word, nothing. What then is the function of the temple, and how is truth at work in this work?

The building incloses the image of a god, and inclosing it lets it stand out within its open space. It presents the

god, and the god's presence makes the temple holy ground.
As long as the god lives here, this holy ground is not
bounded by the walls and columns that are its apparent
limit; it extends beyond. It stretches along the lines and
ways and modes of men's lives. Birth and death, blessing
and disaster, triumph and defeat, joy, endurance, agony,
and ruin—none of these happens without the god. Thus
this ground embraces and unites all the aspects of the life
of a nation and exposes a world to our sight.

The temple stands on rock and its stand reveals the rock
as unyielding support. It endures the storm, and its monumental rest enhances the raging of the elements. Its lines,
clearly detached from the sky, bring forth the latter's
expanse. The gleaming stone that reflects the sun makes
light and darkness apparent. Even tree and grass, eagle and
bull, snake and grasshopper are more what they are for
the temple's stand. Thus the temple promotes the dawn,
growth, and flow of what the Greeks called *physis* and
exposes the all-resisting earth in its self-inclosed self-refusal.
It is a work of art because it opens up a world as its abode,
a world that would not be there but for the openness in
which it stands. Hewn in stone, the work brings the stone
into its own; built on rock, it produces (leads forward, makes
apparent) the earth; reaching toward the clouds, it illuminates the sky. It is a work of art because it gathers the
world—gods and men—and the earth into their unity and
reveals them as what they are. Made by men, made of stone,
it makes (unfolds, brings to light) all. It opens up the rift
between the world and the earth, which, in the strife of
their opposition, lend each other splendor. This strife is
what we call the monumental peace and quiet rest of the
work of art. The peace—or inward strife, agon, war—that
illuminates the face of things and gives men insight into
themselves; the happening of truth. (The preceding three

paragraphs loosely paraphrase the substance of *Holzw* 30–32.)[6]

One thing that is new in this treatment of the happening of truth is the restriction of "world" to men and gods. Opposing the world, there is such a thing as the earth. What is the meaning of this opposition that Heidegger talks about?

The world is still characterized by disclosure. "The work as work erects a world. The work holds open the openness of the world" (*Holzw* 34). But the erection, i.e. disclosure, of the world is not all that happens here. "By ensconcing itself in the bulk and weight of the stone" (*Holzw* 35) the work produces (brings forward) the earth into the openness of the world. It "lets the earth be." In contrast to the world whose *"Welten"* is disclosure, the earth offers a primordial resistance: even in the openness into which it is brought, it is disclosed as that which resists all disclosure, as the undisclosable self-inclosed concealment. "To pro-duce the earth means: to bring it into the open as that which is closed up in itself" (*Holzw* 36).

6. When Heidegger speaks of the rift, strife, and agon that is brought about in and through the work of art, these words are to be understood in the sense of the Heracleitean *polemos* (fr. 53) that is creator and preserver of all. This war or conflict is the original separation and mutual opposition of all that is, through which separation and opposition beings first obtain "status and stand and rank" (*Einf* 47): presence. "In this putting-asunder (*polemos*) or unfolding, world originates" (ibid.). Unity is not destroyed. On the contrary, what is here opposed is gathered into a unity. The unity itself emerges only in the separation in which all that is is joined in a harmony of opposites. This joining or gathering or collection is the function of *polemos* qua *logos*. The artistic *polemos* is a *legein*—bringing together as distinct and thereby laying open to sight—that brings things to a stand, gives them status and presence, makes them appear, and thus brings about beauty, disclosure, truth, Being. On Heidegger's interpretation of Heracleitus' *polemos*, see *Einf* 47–48, 100–01. See also *E* 58 on *Aus-einandersetzung*.

The work, erecting a world (of disclosure) and pro-ducing the earth (the undisclosable), unites them and brings about their inward strife. "The essence of the work consists in enstriving the conflict between world and earth" (*Holzw* 38). The conflict opens up a clearing full of light. The open-ness of the clearing makes the concealment of what is hidden (the earth) apparent, while the concealment of the latter accentuates the openness of the former.

All this is but another way of saying that truth and untruth (disclosure and concealment) belong together. The agon between world and earth (openness and concealment) is the happening of truth-untruth. This happening is the essence of the work of art. "Erecting a world and producing the earth, the work is the enstriving of the conflict in which the disclosure of all that is, i.e. truth, is accomplished" (*Holzw* 44).

In *Being and Time* truth and untruth were relative to modes of Being of Dasein. Dasein was fighting the battle of the steresis (*a-letheia*), and this fight of disclosure was the happening of truth. Now in *Holzwege* we see the same shift of emphasis as we observed in *Of the Essence of Truth*.

Truth is still a strife, tension, and conflict, but the role of Dasein is no longer as obvious as it seemed in *Being and Time*. The "earth" does not stand for merely the unformed bulk (the stone, the clay, or the worn fabric of everyday language) that resists the artist's attempt at transforming and informing it, at eliciting from the self-inclosed material the form that shines forth, disclosed, in beauty. Nor is it just a symbol for the hiddenness of the artist to himself, man's self-concealment, which he tries to overcome in creation, giving himself an image in which he is reflected and on which he can reflect. The strife of truth-untruth is not just the artist's struggle for self- and world-disclosure. It is the world (gods and men) and the earth that are locked in conflict here, and disclosure, no longer based on Dasein as the being whose mode of Being is to be disclosing, is an illumined clearing (*Lichtung*) whose openness is permeated by the hiddenness not of an unauthentic disclosure but of the earth itself as that which remains forever unopen, self-inclosed, mysterious. Dasein, though still a participant in the happening of truth, no longer seems to be the chief protagonist. Its existence no longer embraces the whole plane, but Dasein itself is caught, as it were, on the plane of the strife between world and earth.

Truth still happens in the conflict of disclosure and concealment. But the conflict is now the ultimate, original rift in the fabric of things that establishes an openness, a breach, a gaping, a chasm in Chaos, within which (openness) all that is is disclosed. The openness is not brought about by man, but by truth itself. Truth itself establishes the clearing, and itself within the clearing, and holds it open against the engulfing oppression of untruth, the primordial darkness that threatens to encroach on the clearing and extinguish the light, and has therefore to be overcome if truth is to prevail. Truth—disclosure—belongs to Being, since it is Being that by its nature clears and illuminates the open region that allows for disclosure. But untruth—hiddenness and mystery—also belongs to Being as that out of which Being comes forth into disclosure and into which it may be its fate to sink. Truth is not wrought by man; It happens by Itself. Not by virtue of a mode of Being of Dasein but by grace of Being, by Its nature, on Its own. And the same is true of untruth. It is the original mystery —dark silence—of Being that is partially cleared up by each disclosure and is revealed in each revelation as the darkness, yet to be dispelled, that surrounds the light.

What then is the role of man? Has he no share in the happening of truth? Is not the work of art, after all, man's work, his creation? And is it not significant that speaking of the diverse modes of the happening of truth Heidegger

enumerates diverse modes of *human* action? "Another way
in which truth *is,* is the state-founding act . . . Yet another
way in which truth founds itself is the essential sacrifice.
Yet another way in which truth becomes is the questioning
of thought" (*Holzw* 50). Creative work, state-founding act,
sacrificial deed, and questioning thought are so many modes
of human behavior, and if truth happens in these modes, is
not truth ultimately, in spite of all assertions to the contrary,
still our contribution?

Not in Heidegger, for in all these acts—if one can still
call them such—man is no longer the actor. He is but the
instrument, the scene, as it were, of the happening of truth.
The real actor is truth itself bringing itself about in and
through the existence of man. What is important in the
work of art is not that *it,* the object, was made by so and so,
but that the essence of the work of art, truth, has come into
its own, i.e. that disclosure of Being has taken place. The
work and the maker are but instruments of this event.
The same is true of the "preservers" of the work. (Not the
men or institutions that store and exhibit the works, but
the true preservers who face the work in its gaping
immensity, endure the conflict, and thus stand in the
revelation.) Their standing within the happening of truth
is only instrumental. Creation and preservation are not the
achievement and act of a self-certain, self-positing and self-
creating subject; creative man is, above all, subject to truth.
"The creative act creates the work. But the essence of the
work (truth) is the original source of the essence of creation"
(*N* I, 135).

But if this is so, is man still instrumental—necessary—
for the happening of truth? And is the work? Could not
truth happen, could not Being be revealed without these
instruments? It seems not. Truth, like magic, needs
instruments. "Truth (*is*) only by establishing itself in
something that is" (*Holzw* 57). The form-infused material,

the painting, the poem, etc. are necessary instruments of truth since they are the media of disclosure, the plane, as it were, in which truth is at work. And although it is the original conflict—of truth-untruth itself—which first "projects and unfolds the unheard of, the so far unsaid and unthought of, this conflict is then borne by the creators, the poets, thinkers, statesmen. They cast the block of the work up against the overwhelming sway (of truth) and bring in it the thus disclosed world to a stand" (*Einf* 47). The work is a symbol not only because it brings the world and the earth together in their opposition (*symballein:* to bring, to throw, together), but because it always points beyond itself and brings something other than itself to light in such a way that the work serves best when it itself—this painting or piece of stone—recedes and makes something else (the truth of Being) shine (as *phainomenon to phanotaton*). And so it is with man. It is not man who brings truth about, but it is truth that makes the maker (*poietes*) and lays claim on the preservers. If the work is a project, man is not the projector; it is truth itself that projects itself into the work and summons us into the fray so that we may receive and transmit—but never initiate— disclosure. Man is no longer the measure, no longer the self-certain designer of the world. He is a humble servant claimed by the truth of Being, and engaged by Being for the preservation of its trust: truth. Man is a mere mask through which another power speaks. Man is "the *persona,* the mask of Being" (*WhD* 28).

Divested of the imagery Heidegger is so fond of employing, all this could be expressed in terms more familiar to us, e.g. those of Plato or Hegel. In Plato's *Phaedrus,* art is a madness, the artist is ecstatic, possessed, out of *his* mind; he speaks not on his own but on behalf of the power that possesses him. He is an inspired transmitter and receiver of a more than human insight; poet, actor, and

audience all respond, ecstatically, to the god's sway
(*Phaedrus, Ion*). Hegel's terms are even more appropriate.
The truth or self-disclosure of Being, i.e. the self-revelation
of the Absolute, happens in and through the existence of
Dasein, i.e. the self-consciousness of man. Human history,
the process of man becoming self-conscious—in artistic
experience or otherwise—is the scene of the history (process
of happening) of Spirit, and that is the history of the self-
disclosure of Spirit (since Spirit is Spirit only in its self-
revelation, as in Heidegger Being *is* only in its truth, i.e.
self-disclosure). Heidegger's self-inclosed earth as the
principle of self-refusal (resistance to disclosure) has its
parallel in the "in-itself" of the Hegelian dialectic—the
"mystery of Being" corresponding to the unrevealed Idea
that needs revelation in order to be Spirit; while the world
(gods and men), characterized by openness and disclosure,
recalls Hegel's "for-itself": Spirit (human or Absolute) as
self-reflective, self-manifesting (self-disclosed and self-
disclosing) Being. In both Heidegger and Hegel "great art
and its works are great in their historical emergence and
being only because they accomplish a decisive task within
the historical existence of man: they reveal, in the manner
of the work, what all that is is, and they preserve the
revelation in the work. Art and its work are necessary only
as a way and as an abode of man, in which the truth of
all that is, i.e. the Unconditional, the Absolute, discloses
itself" (*N* I, 100).

These parallels, crude as they are, do less injustice to
Heidegger's thought in *Holzwege* than would seem from
such a brief comparison. I shall let them stand, however,
for the time being, and elaborate on them only when the
time comes for a concluding judgment. One purpose of
reminding the reader of Hegel at this point is to point out
an affinity between *Holzwege* and the *Phenomenology*
which transcends similarity of detail. In the *Phenomenology*

Hegel gave us a magnificent, imaginative story: the history of the self-revelation of Absolute Spirit. In *Holzwege,* and indeed in the majority of his later works, Heidegger is engaged in a similar activity. Starting with the essay on the origin of the work of art, which sets the stage and gives the theme of the whole work, Heidegger presents us with an eschatological history of the truth—self-disclosure— of Being. Plato, Descartes, Hegel; Nietzsche, Hoelderlin, and Rilke; Heracleitus, Parmenides, and Anaximander, all yield to Heidegger's virtuosity in interpretation and become but so many stages in the *parousia* of Being. The fact that Anaximander is the last thinker dealt with in *Holzwege,* and that the pre-Socratic Greeks play an increasingly large role in Heidegger's later thought, does not make the presentation any less eschatological, for Heidegger regards a return to the origins of Greek thought as the best preparation for the "advent" of Being. And all his efforts are directed toward this *eschaton.*

It will not be necessary for us here to follow Heidegger in detail through the stages of his eschatological description. The theme of the whole is given in the earlier résumé of "The Origin of the Work of Art," and it is this theme that is important for us. The problem of this study is the problem of truth. This is also the problem, implicitly or explicitly, of all the essays in *Holzwege.* Since truth is the disclosure of Being, and since one of the modes of the happening of this disclosure is the "thinking of thought," these essays, each dealing with the thought of a thinker, will not only have truth as a subject matter, but in rethinking past thought the thinker—Heidegger—himself will "work truth," i.e. will be the instrument of the self-disclosure of Being. It is in such capacity that Heidegger confronts us in the pages of this work.

"Thinking pronounces the dictate of the truth of Being" (*Holzw* 303). Thus the thinker does not act on his own, but, like Plato's divinely inspired poet or soothsayer, or like the ecstatic enthusiast of Dionysus, he is *entheos,* possessed: he acts on behalf of a power in, above, and beyond himself. Thought is a kind of divine madness, and the thinker like the seer (*ho mantis ho mainomenos*) is distracted, beside himself, in a holy transport. He is distracted from his "everyday sanity," the humdrum joys and cares of his daily life, from the oppression of the things around him, from himself as he is in the public involvement in day to day existence. He is transported away from all this and beyond it into a region free from all this insistent oppression, a region in which he is free, i.e. free for, open to, the disclosure of Being. In this region sight is no longer relative to the eye, but it is relative to, inasmuch as granted by, the illumination (truth) of Being (*Holzw* 322). Thus transported, the seer becomes the preserver of this grant, the surrogate, the shepherd of the truth of Being, and thinking is not so much the thought of man as the "thinking of Being." *"Es braucht uns":* Being needs and uses us for its self-revelation. In this instrumentality lies the essence of man, as Heidegger suggests on the last page of *Holzwege:* "But what if Being, in its essence, *needs* and *uses* the essence of man? What if the essence of man lies in the thinking of the truth of Being?" (*Holzw* 343).[7] This rhetorical question is answered in the later writings in full accordance with the program laid down in the works I have dealt with. "The history of Being is neither the history of man and mankind, nor the history of the human relationship to beings and to Being. The history of Being is Being itself and only this. But because Being claims the essence of man for the grounding of its truth in what is, man remains involved in the history of Being, albeit always only with respect to the way in which, on the basis of Being's relation to him and

7. The italics are Heidegger's; the italicized word *"braucht"* is translated in its double connotation.

in accordance with this relation, he accepts, loses, passes up, relinquishes, fathoms, or dissipates his essence" (*N* I, 489).

The history of man, the history of art, thought, and nature are all but so many aspects of the same: the history—process of unfolding—of the truth of Being. Or is it perhaps paradoxical to speak of a history of nature in the same breath with a history of man? Is not nature supposed to be unhistorical, i.e. precisely the opposite of what we call history? Is nature not the principle of self-refusal, conceal-ment, mystery, i.e. primarily untruth in the Heideggerian sense, and not truth, the disclosure of Being?

It is not. For Heidegger, Kierkegaard's motto truly holds: the time of making distinctions is gone. Having descended into "the poverty of thought" (*Hum* 47) Heidegger has but one subject, and that is the truth of Being. Nature, for him, is not the subject matter of the natural sciences, nor is it the opposite of the world (gods and men): the earth. It is the earth and the skies, men and the gods, the beasts, the trees, and the waters. It is more fundamental than any being, underlying and embracing them all as their ground. It is what the Greeks called *physis*. And *physis* is nothing but the self-revelation of Being.

Truth and Nature

Physis means growth. But growth is not to be understood as evolution, increase, or becoming; growth is "unfolding." It is *phyein* in the sense of unfolding into the open, coming forward into the light, into that light which itself only dawns with the dawn of the unfolding. *Physis* is the re-velation (literally unfolding) or illumination into and within which all that comes to be comes to be. *Physis* is the hearth of all life, the light of all illumination, the original power: *"sie ist das Machtende selbst"* (*E* 52). *Physis* is spirit: it is the original inspiration that inspires all.[8] It is the absolute source and ground of all. "*Physis* is the coming forth and unfolding, the self-opening, which unfolding at the same time returns to its source . . . *Physis,* as a ground-word, means the emergence into the open . . . the emergent return into itself. *Physis* is the dawn of enlightening the enlightened, and thus the hearts and dwelling-place of the light" (*E* 55). *Physis* means *genesis* and *phthora* at the same time; *genesis:* coming forth into light, disclosure; *phthora:* sinking back into concealment (*Holzw,* "Anaximander's Sentence"). *Physis* is the original disclosure, on the ground of which all particular coming to be and passing away is possible. *Physis* is the self-disclosure of Being, the truth of Being, i.e. the happening of *aletheia.* As such it is not opposed to history but is history itself: the happening of the truth of Being.

Having made *physis* one of his "ground-words"—words like *aletheia, logos, physis, phainesthai, noein, einai,* which are, as we shall see, only so many names for the same thing and can be used interchangeably—Heidegger never tires of reverting to it in the attempt to reinforce the above interpretation. In the *Holzwege* essays on Rilke and Anaximander, in the Hoelderlin essays, in the *Introduction to Metaphysics,* in *Vortraege und Aufsaetze,* and in the essay on Aristotle's concept of *physis,* we again and again find the word translated in almost literally the same terms. *Physis* is "self-opening unfolding, and, by way of this unfolding, it is entrance into, standing within, and persistence in appearing. In short, *physis* is unfolding-abiding sway" (*Einf* 11). "*Physis* is Being itself . . ." (ibid.). It is the "in-itself-abiding self-unfolding" in which "*aletheia* happens" and "world is accomplished" (*Einf* 47). Far from being opposed to history, *physis* qua "world-genesis is history in the authentic sense of the word" (*Einf* 48). It is

8. "*sie ist selbst 'die Begeisterung.' Be-geistern kann sie nur weil sie 'der Geist' ist*" (*E* 58).

"world epiphany" (ibid.): epiphany, *phainesthai, aletheia,* in the sense of a self-manifestation of Being. *Physis* and *phainesthai* are the same, for "the roots *phy-* and *pha-* name the same thing. *Phyein,* the unfolding that rests in itself, is *phainesthai,* shining forth, self-manifesting, appearing" (*Einf* 77). "Being *is* as *physis*" (ibid.). *Physis* is *aletheia* (*Einf* 78). Being is *physis* (*Einf* 79).[9] Being, *physis, phainesthai,* and *aletheia* are the same.

It is instructive to compare this interpretation of *physis* (*aletheia, phainesthai,* Being) with Heidegger's interpretation of Plato's *agathon* as presented in *Of the Essence of the Ground,* an essay written soon after *Being and Time.* In that essay, *to agathon* occupied the place of what is now called *physis;* it was the "original power," the ground of all truth, understanding, and Being, "the ground of the possibility of the truth of the understanding of Being" (*G* 37). On the face of it the change from *agathon* to *physis* seems a harmless substitution of one concept for another. But if we recall that the disclosure of Being in *Being and Time* and *Of the Essence of the Ground* was "the primordial act of human existence" (*G* 37), and, as this original act— also called the transcendence of Dasein—it was "primordial history," i.e. the happening of the truth of Being, we can see the difference inherent in the substitution. To understand *to agathon* as the transcendence of Dasein (*G* 37), and to conceive of transcendence as the original power, the ground, the primordial history (the happening of the truth) of Being, is to make human existence the ground of all disclosure, and as such the ground of Being itself. This is an extreme radicalization of all humanism, the attempt to make man the absolute center of all, and thus the direct opposite of the position Heidegger takes in the later essays.

With the about-face in the latter, man is no longer

9. See also *Vortr* 19, 49, 263; *Ar* 56.

cosmically displaced and utterly homeless—it was precisely his becoming the ground of all that made it impossible to find a ground for him—but is himself grounded in something more original than his own existence. In the humble role of the preserver, the shepherd of the truth of Being, he obtains a new home, which, not being self-given, rests on a more secure foundation than the one established by the self-certainty of the self-certain subject. The void created by the "death of God," proclaimed by Nietzsche's madman, could not be filled by man himself, and so Heidegger now takes recourse to something totally beyond the sphere of immanent human jurisdiction and infinitely more powerful than the transcendence of Dasein, of which it is the ground: to *physis* as the process of the self-revelation of self-granting and self-revealing Being. It is this recourse that is expressed by the substitution of *physis* for *agathon*. And the resultant shift of emphasis from Dasein to Being is reinforced with every step that carries Heidegger farther and farther on his somber "paths in the wood" (Holzwege).

Truth and Thought

We have already seen (pp. 103–105) that for Heidegger "thinking pronounces the dictate of the truth of Being," that the thinker is possessed (by and for the truth of Being), and that thought is a mode of the happening of the truth of Being. We observed Heidegger reducing thought to the "thinking of Being" and raising questions concerning the instrumentality of man as a thinking being. "Is it perhaps the case that the essence of man is instrumental for the essence of Being?" Is the essence of man anything but "the thinking of the truth of Being?" Confronted with these assertions and questions we must now devote some time to reflecting on the nature of thought in Heidegger.

What is thought? This question can be best answered by

letting Heidegger himself speak. In his later writings he dealt with the problem of thought repeatedly, and I shall try to present here the substance of his discussions in *Was ist Metaphysik?*[10], *Ueber den Humanismus, Was heisst Denken?, Einfuehrung in die Metaphysik,* and *Vortraege und Aufsaetze.*

In the "Postscript" to *What Is Metaphysics?* we read the following sentence: "But supposing that not only does all that is derive from Being, but that also, and even more originally, Being itself rests in its truth and the truth of Being *is* (*west*) as the Being of truth, then it is necessary to ask the question what is metaphysics in its origin (*WiM* 40). The meaning of this sentence becomes clearer if we think truth in the Greek (*aletheia:* disclosure). "The truth of Being *is* as the Being of truth," or (as the same thing was expressed in *Of the Essence of Truth,* "Postscript" 1943) "the essence of truth is the truth of essence" (*WW* 26), means that the essence of truth is the disclosure of Being as such. Being is disclosed, the disclosure of Being happens, as the essential happening of truth, i.e. as the happening of the disclosure of Being. In this translation the sentence pronounces a tautology. But if we read the proposition "the essence of truth is the disclosure of Being" together with the one before it, "originally Being itself rests in its truth," then the two together assert that Being itself rests in its disclosure, that the essence of Being is the disclosure of Being, i.e. that Being *is* its disclosure or self-revelation. *Being is truth.* As such the sentence becomes significant, and we can understand why the rest—"it is necessary . . . ," etc.—follows and what it means. Let us repeat part of the sentence once more. "But supposing that not only does all that is derive from Being, but that also, and even more

10. "Postscript" (1943) and "Introduction" (1949) only. The essay itself, written in 1929, belongs to Heidegger's *Being and Time* period.

originally, Being itself rests in its truth . . . then it is necessary
to ask the question what is metaphysics in its origin."

We have seen that in his later writings Heidegger
criticized metaphysics for being an investigation of beings
and their categories of Being that is so preoccupied with
categorizing that it fails to think of that which is more
fundamental than any and all beings, namely, Being itself.
Even *Being and Time* could not quite overcome this oblivion
of truth and Being because of its humanistic orientation,
i.e. because it considered man, rather than Being, the
ultimate source of metaphysics. But now, "Supposing that
all that is derives from Being," we have to reevaluate
metaphysics by going to its ground. The ground of
metaphysics—that which makes metaphysics possible—is,
since Kant, the same as the ground of the possibility of the
objects of metaphysics. In *Being and Time* this still seemed
to be human Dasein characterized by a disclosure of Being.
In *What Is Metaphysics?*, however, it is no longer Dasein;
it is Being as the ground of all disclosure, Being as
primordial disclosure, Being as self-disclosure. In other
words, the source of metaphysics is the happening of truth:
aletheia as the self-disclosure of Being.

But if all Western metaphysics failed to get at Being
itself, how are we now to think of the truth of Being? How
are we to think in such a manner that our thought becomes
the thought, i.e. self-revelation, of Being, i.e. becomes that
which for Heidegger it essentially is? To learn this we have
to ask the question: what is thought?

Thought thinks Being. "But Being is not a product of
thought. On the contrary, essential thought is an event of
Being" (*WiM* 43). "Event" is not to be understood here
in the usual sense of the word. It means both event (*e-venire:*
to come out) and advent (*ad-venire:* to come to, to arrive).
Thought is the event of the coming (out into the open,
arriving and establishing itself in the light) of Being. It is

that event in which Being is disclosed. It is the event of the truth of Being, the event in which Being happens (is disclosed) unto us in order that we "spend ourselves for the preservation of the truth of Being" (*WiM* 44). Original thought is the "echo of the favor (i.e. the event) of Being" (ibid.) and as this echo it is the answer (of man) to the call of Being, which (call, the event, the favor) claims man (his essence, his *humanitas*) for its (Being's) own truth (disclosure). Thought is the "grace" of Being (Being granting itself) and the "sacrifice" of man (man spending himself in answer to the call) for the disclosure of Being. But this self-sacrifice is such that man gains all and loses nothing by it: it is in and through it alone that man first obtains a self he can sacrifice, for man's self, his essence, his humanity, lies in preserving the disclosure of Being. The origin of thought—that which brings thought on its way—is not man, but the origin of both thought and man is that "which is to be thought," i.e. Being itself.

Thought is action. But to act means to accomplish, and "to accomplish means to unfold something in (to) the fullness of its essence, to lead it forward into this, *producere*. Therefore, only that can be accomplished that already is. But what 'is' above all, is Being. Thought accomplishes the relation of Being to the essence of man. It does not make or effect this relationship. It only renders it unto Being as that (relationship) which has been bestowed upon it by Being" (*Hum* 5). The relationship is rendered, offered up to Being, so that Being may come to word. The word—language—is the "house of Being," inhabited by man as the guardian of this dwelling, i.e. the guardian of the disclosure of Being in thought and word.

Thought is not an action by virtue of its having practical results. "Thinking acts insofar as it thinks. This act is presumably the simplest and at the same time the highest of all actions, because it concerns the relationship of Being

to man" (ibid.), a relationship which is man's essence. The
ground of all effective action is Being. Thought, in yielding
to Being, is engaged by Being for saying the truth of Being.
"Thinking is the engagement by Being for Being." It is "the
engagement of Being" (ibid.) if the genitive is taken to be
both objective and subjective genitive at the same time.
"Thought, to put it simply, is the thought of Being. The
genitive expresses two things at once. Thought is the thought
of Being, insofar as thought, effected by Being, belongs to
Being. Thought is, at the same time, the thought of Being
insofar as thought, belonging to Being, hearkens to Being."
(*Hum* 7). "Belonging to Being, since thrown by Being into
the preservation of its truth and engaged by Being in this
task, it (thought) thinks Being" (*Hum* 42).

Since what is accomplished in thinking is nothing but
the truth of Being, accomplished by Being itself rather than
man, thought is neither theoretical nor practical. It is more
fundamental than either theory or practice. Thinking the
truth of Being, thought is the light which makes all sight
and vision (*theoria*) possible and accomplishes the act—
the disclosure of Being—which is the ground of all
(practical) action. Thought as an act is most like an act
of devotion: it is "the devotion to Being, and nought else"
(ibid.).

The quasi-biblical tone of Heidegger's pronouncements
is quite appropriate to what he is trying to say. For in his
conception of thought—as thought by Being, for Being,
and of Being—the importance of the thinker as a self-certain
subject is as much reduced as it is in the biblical conception
of revelation—of God, by God, and for the greater glory
of God. At the same time, just as in and through biblical
revelation, man obtains a new dignity as the preserver of
the truth of Being, called by Being into the preservation
of its truth. Although thought is no longer an adventurous
search in which man opens up new, unknown, and

unthought of regions on his own, it is still an adventure in the sense that it is the "advent" of Being. Although it is no longer man's project, it is still a project, namely the self-projection (self-revelation) of Being. This self-projection or self-committing mission and destiny of Being is the history of the truth of Being, happening in the thought of man. "Being has already committed (bestowed, allotted, *zugeschickt*) itself to thought. Being *is* as the mission (fate, destiny, *Geschick*) of thought. This mission is inherently historical. Its history has already come to word through the utterances of thinkers" (*Hum* 46).

In Greek terminology, it makes little difference to Heidegger whether he says *"moira* is the mission of Being" (*Vortr* 252), Being is the *moira* of thought, or thought is the *moira* of Being. *Moira* means allotment, distribution, apportionment, and the lot, fate, and portion allotted. "Being is the *moira* of thought" would have the double meaning that Being *is* only insofar as it allots, contributes, commits itself to thought, and that the allotted portion and function, the essential nature of thought, is to think of Being. "Thought is the *moira* of Being" would mean both that thought is the grant (self-contribution) of Being, that only insofar as Being entrusts itself to thought can thinking be, and that essential thought, the disclosure of Being, is the *moira* (nature, essence, fate) of Being, since only insofar as thought is can Being be (i.e. be disclosed). Essential thought (the disclosure of Being) and Being belong together, fatefully. That is why, even in Greek, essential thought is full of *aidos:* awe-ful reverence (see "Moira," in *Vortr* 251–55).

To utter the *moira,* mission, advent, or event of Being, is "the sole task of thought. That is why essential thinkers say forever the same" (*Hum* 47). This "sameness" is certainly noticeable in Heidegger's writings, for the preceding analysis of the nature of thought leaves us exactly where we were at the end of his discussions of the nature of truth (*WW*), the essence of the work of art, and nature (*Holzw*). Thought has turned out to be but another name for what Heidegger previously called freedom, truth, art, history, *physis, phainesthai* or Being. All these names refer to the same: the disclosure of Being, by Being, for the sake of Being. The progressive identification of fundamental terms, "ground-words" whose meaning is ultimately reduced to the same ground, the truth of Being, is a striking characteristic—one might almost say the aim—of Heidegger's later philosophy. This philosophy consists of nothing but a long succession of variations on a theme, and, after a while, the reader begins to wonder whether there have been any variations at all, or if only the selfsame theme keeps returning under a variety of titles. Heidegger is by no means resistant to such a suggestion, for, conscious of the underlying theme, he insists on it and repeatedly expresses that his whole philosophy has but one subject: the truth of Being. "Every thinker thinks only one single thought . . . The thinker needs only one single thought. And the thinker's difficulty consists in holding fast this single, this one thought as the only one that is for him to think, in thinking this one as the same, and in speaking of this same one in the appropriate manner. But we speak of the same in the manner appropriate to it only when we always say the same of the same, in such a way that thereby we are used by the same. Thus, for thought, the limitlessness of the same is the sharpest limit" (*WhD* 20). This "limitlessness of the same" accounts for the unity, overall harmony, and grand monotony of Heidegger's thought after *Being and Time*. *Holzwege* is an apt title not only for the particular collection of essays it has been chosen for, but, indeed, for all of Heidegger's later writings. They are but so many somber paths in the wood, all alike though perhaps none quite the same. It seems to be of little importance which one one takes, for none of them leads out of this primordial forest; if possible, they lead us in deeper and deeper. It is also possible that they are all circular. What Heidegger hopes is that they are each a clearing letting in some light.

It is not without reason that Heidegger admires the splendid simplicity of pre-Socratic thought. He shares with the early Greeks a characteristic that he believes modern philosophy lacks and needs most: a "poverty of thought." His remark concerning Heraclitus, that in the Ephesian's philosophy "Being is *logos, harmonia, aletheia, physis, phainesthai*" (*Einf* 102), is so descriptive of his own thought that one hardly knows where to stop in enumerating terms that are identical in meaning for him. We have seen this when dealing with his interpretation of *physis*—as *aletheia, phaiensthai,* Being—and now we have to add to the list thought, or *logos,* too. "*Physis* and *logos* are the same" (*Einf* 100), "*aletheia* and *logos* are the same" (*Vortr* 220). *Logos* is *apophainesthai* (*Vortr* 213); the disclosure of that which shows itself as it shows itself by itself, i.e. the disclosure of Being.[11] *Logos* is Being, i.e. its own self-disclosure in thought. Since all of Heidegger's thought is directed toward making Being itself once again "thought-worthy" (problematic and worth being thought about) he believes his gradual "descent into the poverty of thought" to be the only way that leads to his goal.

We shall accompany Heidegger on one last lap of his descent. In *Was heisst Denken?* he raises the question "What is thought?" once again. Although he does not answer the question directly here, he keeps raising it in different ways in such a manner that the answer reveals itself as implicit in the question. This answer is important for us

11. Compare *Being and Time,* §7.

because *Was heisst Denken?* is one of Heidegger's latest writings[12] and as such it enables us to see if his conception of thought—and of truth and Being—has changed since the publication of *Holzwege* and the *Letter on Humanism.*

"Was heisst Denken?"[13] The question, as it is put in German, may be interpreted in four major ways. It may mean: 1. What does the word "thinking" refer to, what is named by this name? It may also mean: 2. How has thought been interpreted in the history of philosophy; what are the traditional conceptions and definitions of "thinking"? It may mean: 3. What belongs to correct thinking, how should we think if we are to think in the right way? And finally: 4. What is it that calls, summons, compels us (*heisst uns*) to think?

All four versions of the question belong together; the answer to one version depends on and indicates the answers to the other three. It may be, however, that one of these questions is more fundamental than the others, and Heidegger, asserting that this is so, proceeds to ask *"Was heisst Denken?"* in the fourth, the "most fundamental" sense.

It is interesting to observe that although Heidegger's answers to all four versions may always have been basically the same, he has not always shown a marked preference for asking the fourth one. In Being and Time we find the first three versions but not the fourth (e.g. the first and second in the analysis of the meaning of *logos* and *phainomenon,* the third in the discussion of authenticity), and, on the whole, *Being and Time* is dominated by a synthesized version of the three. The question "What is Being?" boils down to "What is the meaning of Being for man?", and the analysis concentrates on Dasein's understanding of Being, on how

12. It is the text of a lecture course given at Freiburg in 1951–52, published in 1954.

13. The following is a summary of the main argument in part 2 of *Was heisst Denken?*

Dasein is constituted so as to have an understanding of
Being, and not—what would be the fourth version—on how
Being constitutes Dasein as an understanding of Being. The
second version—answering the question by way of a historical interpretation—can be found in *Of the Essence of the
Ground* and *Of the Essence of Truth,* and it becomes pre-
dominant in *Holzwege* and some of the later essays. In the
Letter on Humanism and in the introduction to *What Is
Metaphysics?,* the reduction of the first three versions to
the fourth becomes apparent, and the fourth version remains in the foreground in all the essays written since that
time. This progressive shift of emphasis—from an emphasis on man to one on Being—indicates, to a certain extent,
the change in the direction of Heidegger's thought since
Being and Time.

At first, the question *"Was heisst Denken?"* seems rather
harmless. We are asking for some information about the
nature of thought, we make thought our topic of discussion,
thought becomes the object—subject matter—of our investigation. Thought is a psychical process in man, man participates in thought, accomplishes the process, so to say. All
this is natural, and we can be quite scientific and theoretical
when dealing with such a natural phenomenon. But the
fourth version of the question, Heidegger believes, undoes
this seeming harmlessness, and bares the question in all its
acute imminence. Asking "what calls us into thought," we
are asking for something that—calling and summoning us
—concerns us so vitally that, with all our scientific remote-
ness and indifference gone, we are ourselves literally in
question. The question strikes home. (This, of course, was
already the case in *Being and Time,* where we were ourselves
in question, too.)

To see exactly what the question *"Was heisst (uns) denken?"* means, let us concentrate on the word *"heissen,"*
which is so ambiguous as to allow all the four different inter-

pretations. *"Heissen,"* like the English "call," means to
summon (in call to order, to duty), to desire, long for (call
for), to appeal to, to invoke, refer, or assign. And all this is
meant here, with an overtone not of commanding but of
desiring, longing for, and entreating. *"Heissen"* means,
furthermore, to bring something on its way, to put something in motion by desiring that it should happen, in the
sense of the Latin *iubere* in the Vulgate (*videns autem Iesus
turbam . . . iussit ire trans fretum,* Matt. 8:18) or the Greek
keleuein (*ho Iesous . . . ekeleusen apelthein,* Matt. 8:18) or
the Sanskrit equivalent which means "to invite." *Heissen*
means also to bid, enjoin, charge, commend, consign,
entrust, and commit, so that the call is at the same time a
commission and a commitment, an obligation and a promise.

Thus, if we ask the question *"Was heisst denken?"* we are
asking a number of questions: What is it that calls (entreats,
desires) and bids us to think, entrusting thought to us, making thought our commitment and making our essence the
preservation of this trust? What is it that commits itself to
us (in thought) by enjoining us to think? What is it that
needs thought by its nature, that needs to be thought, i.e.
needs to be accomplished, sustained, and preserved by
thought?

Whatever it is that calls us to thought, it gives us, as we
see, enough to consider. This could not be otherwise, for it
is that which is most "considerable" and "thought-worthy";
it is that which by nature most requires thoughtful consideration. As such, whatever consigns us to thought commits to
us, at the same time, itself as that which is to be thought. In
entrusting us with thinking it gives us no less a trust than
Itself. What we are entrusted by and what we are entrusted
with are the same: that which calls us to thought (*WhD* 85).

Having been entrusted with this trust we preserve it (by
thinking). But even this preservation is not something ex-
traneous to that which, needing to be thought, calls us into

thinking. The preservation of the trust itself belongs to the Caller as Its essential mode of giving and granting Itself. Man merely lives in and for and as the preservation of that which grants him thought; he does not originate the preservation (*WhD* 97). "Original thought" has a seemingly transcendent origin.

I shall not deal here with Heidegger's answer to the first version of the question *"Was heisst Denken?"* (What does the word "thinking" refer to ?), because this answer, analyzing the meaning of thinking (into *Denken, Gedachtes, Gedaechtnis, Gedanc, Dank,* etc.), is not novel in Heidegger. Thinking is "thanking" for the trust of thought, which thanking (thinking) preserves the trust of and for that which granted (itself in) thought because it needed to be thought. It will be more illuminating to present the argument of Heidegger in which he tries to show that even though the pre-Socratic Greeks had not explicitly raised the question *"Was heisst denken?"* in the fourth sense, they had been aware of this meaning of the question. They did not ask, what is it that calls us to think?, but they had done something more appropriate than merely to raise the question: they were conscious of the call and responded to it by simple, original thought in such a manner that, in their thought, that which summoned them to thinking came to light.

A Parmenidean fragment begins with the words: *chre to legein te noein t'eon emmenai.* These words are what Heidegger undertakes to interpret to support his argument.

The fragment is usually translated as "It is necessary to say and to think that what is is." Heidegger orders the paratactic sentence as *chre: to legein te noein t': eon: emmenai*—"Necessary: the saying as well as the thinking: being: to be"—and he proceeds to translate the words *chre, legein, noein, eon,* and *emmenai* in a way he believes to be less alien to Parmenides' way of thinking than the standard translation given above.

Chre belongs to the verb *chrao, chraomai,* related to *cheir* (the hand). *Chrao, chraomai* mean to handle, to have in hand, to hold and keep in hand, to use, to employ. But "to put to a use, to make use of, to use to one's advantage" are, according to Heidegger, only derivative meanings of *chresthai*. The authentic meaning of "use" involves an appropriate employment suited to the nature of what is used. "Use" does not consume, exhaust, or debase that which is used; on the contrary, it lets it be what it is, engages it in what is suited to its nature (the nature of what is used), installs it in its essence and holds it there, thus preserving and fulfilling the essence of what is used. Use means implementation (from *implere:* to fill in, to fulfill) by essentially suitable employment (from *implicare:* to unfold in its essence), in and through which (use) the essence of what is used is brought to light. Let us hold on to the preceding interpretation of *chre* or *es brauchet* as "there is use" in the sense of "there is entrance into and preservation of essence" (*WhD* 114–19) and take the next words in the sentence, *legein* and *noein*.

The dictionary translation of *legein* is: to say, to tell, to relate. But *legein* has the same root as *"legere," "legen," "lay";* and that is what "say" means. To "say" is to "lay," i.e. to present, to offer, to put forward, lay open, and let lie in the open. When we "say" something (of something) we present it (as such and such) and let it appear (as such). This *legein,* the original say and lay, is the *logos* (lay) that brings something to light, lays it open and makes it apparent by letting it lie in the open. The *legein* of *logos* is the *apophainesthai* of *apophansis,* the *aletheuein* of *aletheia* (*WhD* 119–24).

We shall be nearer to the original meaning of *noein,* too, if we do not translate it right away as "to think" but render it more cautiously as "to perceive, to apprehend." Perceive and apprehend are to be understood here not in the sense of an altogether passive reception but as an acceptance that is at the same time an inception, i.e. one that incepts, undertakes, begins to do something with what is perceived, i.e. received and accepted. But what do we do with what we perceive, receive, and accept inceptively in *noein?* We mind it, not only by obeying it in accepting it, but also in the sense of heeding and tending it, attending to it, taking it in our care and custody. This "minding acceptance in our care" is the essence of *noein* (*WhD* 124–25).

If we translate *legein* and *noein* as we have just done, it becomes apparent why and in what manner *legein* precedes *noein* in the Parmenides fragment. The sequence of words is by no means fortuitous: *legein* precedes *noein* not only because it is presupposed by the latter, i.e. because *noein* can "accept in care" only that which *legein* lays open and brings to light, but also because it goes beyond the latter: *legein*—in the sense of *legere, colligere,* to collect—gathers that which is taken in care by *noein* and preserves it in its togetherness. Thus *legein* and *noein* are not isolated words in the fragment but are joined together. *Legein* is essentially directed toward *noein,* while *noein* itself is a sort of *legein:* taking whatever is brought to light by *legein* in its care, *noein* preserves the light (and that which is brought to light as it is brought to light), and by preserving it offers (lays) it back to *legein* so that *legein,* as a kind of *noein* (*concapere, concipere, colligere*), might gather it all in its togetherness and preserve it. This relation of interdependence and essential interchange between *legein* and *noein* is expressed by Parmenides' combining them in *legein te noein te.*

Conceived in this way, the fragment is most illuminating, because it does not so much presuppose a definition of thought as it indicates what are the fundamental traits, the original nature, of that which we have come to know under the name of "thinking." *Legein* and *noein* joined together accomplish what for a short while the Greeks called *aletheuein:* the disclosure and preservation of the disclosure of what is disclosed (*WhD* 125–26).

But even the essential combination of *legein* and *noein* as *aletheuein* fails to define the nature of thought completely, because the combination itself is not complete but refers to something else that would complete it. "Bringing to light" and "accepting in care" (*legein-noein*) can be fully defined only if we know what it is that *legein* and *noein* are concerned with. In Parmenides *legein te noein te* is followed by *eon emmenai*. These words ought to tell us something about thought that could complete our description.

Great care must be taken in translating these two words, whose meaning, completing the definition of thought, is to supply the answer to our question *"Was heisst Denken?"* At the moment all we know is that *legein* and *noein* refer to *eon emmenai;* there is some sort of relation between them. The relation cannot be accidental, i.e. one that may or may not obtain, for Parmenides says *"chre":* there is essential use, there is installation, implementation, and preservation of essence. Whose essence is fulfilled in the relation of *legein* and *noein* to *eon emmenai?* Does thought (as *legein* and *noein*) essentially need beings and Being, or do beings need thought in their essence, i.e. in order to be? Are *eon* and *emmenai* the "object" of thought or is Being the "subject" that essentially needs and thus unfolds thought? Or, finally, is it possible that there is a relation of interdependence and mutually essential need between *legein-noein* and *eon emmenai?* Can it be that *eon* or *emmenai* or the two together call thinking into its essence, which is precisely the relation of *legein-noein* to *eon emmenai,* and that this relation comes about essentially, i.e. because it is the essence of *eon emmenai* to call thinking (*legein-noein*) into the relation? This would actually answer our question "What calls us into thinking?," and it is not surprising that Heidegger interprets Parmenides as saying precisely this. If this is the case, however, there is all the more need to understand what *eon emmenai* means.

Parmenides groups the participle *eon* (being) and the infinitive *emmenai* (to be) together and the purely grammatical form of these words already gives us an indication of what he is driving at. *Legein* and *noein* are concerned with *eon* with respect to its *emmenai:* they accept all beings (*eonta*) in their care and attend to the Being (*emmenai*) of what is. *Chre to legein te noein te eon emmenai* thus announces the perennial program of all metaphysics: there is essential use in thinking—thinking corresponds to its own essence—only when thought attends to the Being of beings, when it goes beyond (*meta*) beings (*ta physika onta*) and concerns itself with the Being of all that is (*WhD* 136). But what did Parmenides mean by being (*eon*) and Being (*emmenai*)?

Heidegger translates *eon* as "that which is present" (*das Anwesende*), and *einai* or *emmenai* as "to be present." Compared with the usual translation of *eon* as *ens, Seiendes,* being, whatever is, and of *einai* or *emmenai* as *esse, Sein,* to be, this is a delimitation of meaning and as such a more specific definition. But even if for the Greeks *einai* and *emmenai* meant *pareinai* (to be present), what have we gained by substituting presence for Being? Heidegger's answer is that the Greeks understood *einai* as *pareinai* with reference to *apeinai* (pre-sence with reference to ab-sence), and that they meant the *para* and *apo* (at, in, with and off, out of, away) to refer not to man but to *aletheia,* i.e. disclosure, revelation, unconcealment. *Pareinai* and *apeinai* thus signified presence in and absence from, entrance into and departure from disclosure and disclosedness (*WhD* 141–44).

What happens now if we understand *eon emmenai* in this sense? In Parmenides' sentence, *to legein te noein te* has an

essential relation (*chre*) to *eon emmenai* because the essence
of thought is grounded in the relation and because the *eon
emmenai* claims the *legein te noein te* as its own and for its
own sake. This means that thought, the "bringing to light
and taking in care," fulfills its essence only as long as it is
directed toward *eon emmenai* (i.e. brings *it* to light and
cares for its disclosure). In other words, the essence of
thought is to bring to light and preserve in disclosure the
presence of what is present in disclosure. But since *chre,*
the essential use, or installation, implementation, and
preservation of essence, refers to *eon emmenai* as well as
to *legein te noein te,* it is not enough to say that the essence
of thought lies in thinking *"eon emmenai."* One also has to
add that the essence of *eon emmenai* is fulfilled only insofar
as it calls thinking into its essence (the relation).

Let us repeat, then, the sentence of Parmenides, and
translate it on the basis of the preceding. *Chre to legein te
noein t'eon emmenai* says: There is an unfolding and
fulfilling of the essence of thought in bringing to light and
preserving the presence of what is present in disclosure.
The presence, in disclosure, of what is present requires
essentially that the essence of thought—the preservation
of the disclosure of what is disclosed—be fulfilled. Being
needs thought as the unfolding of the disclosure of Being
essentially, i.e. since the essence of Being is disclosure.
In an already familiar formulation the sentence says: The
essence of thought is the disclosure of Being accomplished
by Being for its own sake. Thought is the disclosure of
Being, for Being, by Being.

It is in this sense that Heidegger interprets Parmenides'
to gar auto noein estin te kai einai. Instead of translating
the fragment in the usual manner, as "thinking and Being
are the same," he explains it: thought and Being essentially
belong together since the essence of thought is the disclosure

of Being while the essence of Being is its self-disclosure in thought. "To be means to stand in the light, to appear, to enter into disclosure. Where this happens, i.e. where Being obtains, there (thought too) obtains and happens concurrently as belonging to Being" (*Einf* 106; see also *WhD* 146–49). Being and thought belong together, since Being *is* its self-disclosure in thought. This is Heidegger's answer to the question *"Was heisst denken?"*, What is it that calls us into thought by calling upon us so that we may think and thus preserve the trust—the disclosure of Being— whose preservation is thought, our essence? That which calls upon us and summons us into thought is the self-disclosure of Being, entrusted to us as our essence, by the call of Being.

This interpretation of Parmenides gives us an answer to the three other versions, too. The first version, "What is the meaning of the word 'thinking'?" is answered: thinking is *legein te noein t'einai:* the accomplishment and preservation of the disclosure of Being. The second version is at least partly answered, since the meaning of thought has been defined by way of a reflection on at least one moment in the history of thought. The answer to the third version, "How are we to think if we are to think in the right manner?", follows from the definition of thought as *legein te noein t'eon emmenai. Chre:* there is essential use, i.e. thinking is accomplished in the way required by the essence of thought, if and only if thinking is directed toward, opens up, cares for, and preserves the disclosure of Being. The second reference of *chre,* namely to *eon emmenai,* answers, as we have seen, the fourth version. *Chre:* it belongs to the essence of *eon emmenai,* i.e. the disclosure of Being, to call thought into its essence, the preservation of this disclosure. It is Being itself that essentially, i.e. by its nature, claims our essence for its own self-disclosure.

Truth and Man

It is time now to return to the problem raised earlier
in this study, namely, whether Heidegger's later thought
escapes the "humanization of truth" that is, according to
him, characteristic of Western metaphysics. Prima facie, we
can answer this question affirmatively on the basis of the
preceding discussion of Heidegger's later writings. Truth,
as the self-disclosure of Being, is no longer humanistic,
since it is no longer the accomplishment of the self-certain
subject as the ultimate ground of all truth and certainty.
It is, rather, the accomplishment of Being whose essence
is precisely this accomplishment of self-disclosure, i.e. the
happening of truth. But if this is so, the essence of man has
to be redefined and brought in line with this new definition
of the essence of truth. In *Being and Time,* truth and Being
were defined relative to and on the basis of a definition of
human existence. Now we have to do the opposite of this
and define the humanity of man on the basis of the self-
disclosure of Being as the relation of Being to man. This
was the program Heidegger announced in *Nietzsche* (I,
358–61) and in the *Introduction to Metaphysics* (pp. 106–
08), and the task is carried out in the *Letter on Humanism,*
where Heidegger reinterprets *Being and Time* in an attempt
to reconcile it with his later thought. "Standing within the
disclosure of Being, that is what I call the existence of man"
(*Hum* 13), Heidegger now announces, and this new definition, according to what he now says, does not really conflict
with the sentence in *Being and Time:* "The essence of
Dasein lies in its existence" (*BT* 42/67). The latter is now
reinterpreted to mean: "Man *is* in such a manner that he is
the 'there,' i.e. the illumination of Being. This 'being' of
the there, and only this, has the fundamental character of
ec-sistence, i.e. of standing ecstatically within the truth of

Being" (*Hum* 15). Ec-sistence is not the medieval *existentia*
as *actualitas,* or the Kantian phenomenal reality in the
sense of objectivity of experience, or Hegel's self-cognizant
idea of absolute subjectivity, or even Nietzsche's eternal
return of the same. Ec-sistence means to "stand within the
truth of Being and to preserve in this stand the essence of
one's Being" (*Hum* 15). Man's essence, ec-sistence, is
literally the "standing out into the truth of Being" (*Hum*
16). Ec-sistence "is the name for that which man is within
the happening of truth" (ibid.). "In ec-sisting, man endures
his *Da-sein* (being-there) by taking the "there," the disclosure of Being, in his care" (ibid.). Ec-sistence is "the
ecstatic relation to the disclosure of Being" (*Hum* 17).

The "ecstatic" character of existence is repeatedly
stressed by Heidegger in an effort to make clear that in
ec-sistence man is beside and beyond himself, beyond the
subjectivity of the self-certain subject, exposed—in *ec-
stasis,* ec-sistence, standing out—into the disclosure of
Being, which he did not create but into which he has been
summoned. Man is no longer in possession, in control, of
himself, let alone of beings and Being. He is possessed by
Being for its disclosure. This possession or *ec-stasis* is the
essence of human ec-sistence. This is why it is so wrong to
focus one's vision on man and his subjectivity when trying
to understand what the essence of man is. On the contrary,
one must turn away from the subject and turn toward that
to which ec-sistence is open and within which ec-sistence
stands: the disclosure of Being. In order to achieve this
dimension one must first of all think of the relation of
Being to man. This relation is the ec-sistence of man, "the
ecstatic stand within the truth of Being" (*Hum* 19).

The definition of the essence or substance of man as
"ec-sistence," Heidegger insists, does not contradict or
invalidate the traditional humanistic definitions of man's
essence. It is, however, opposed to them, because defining

man as a rational animal, as a person, as a rational-psychi-
cal-corporeal being, etc. "does not set the humanity of man
high enough" and fails to express "the proper dignity of
man" (*Hum* 19). "Man is what he is essentially only when
addressed by Being" (*Hum* 13). His dignity is not that of
a subject that rules over all beings by positing them in his
role of *metron panton*. If the characterization of Dasein as
"projecting" has led many to conceive of Dasein in *Being
and Time* as the epitome of the self-certain subject,
Heidegger can only deplore this in the *Letter on Humanism*.
The emphasis, then and now, must be placed on Being,
for "man is 'thrown' by Being itself into the truth of Being
in order that by ec-sisting in this manner he preserve the
truth of Being, so that in the light of Being whatever is
might appear as it is" (*Hum* 19). Man does not decide what
beings and in what manner beings appear in this light; this
is altogether beyond his power. "The advent of that which
is" (ibid.) depends on the event and advent of Being, i.e.
on the way Being comes to us granting itself in disclosure.
Man's essence lies only in taking this grant in his care
and thus preserving the truth of Being "by ec-sisting within
it." This is why in *Being and Time* man's mode of Being
was experienced as "Care"—according to what Heidegger
says now. Man is not the lord of the universe, he is the
"shepherd of Being" (ibid.). And Being is not God. "Being
is Itself" (ibid.). It is "more embracing than all beings and,
at the same time, nearer to man than any being" (ibid.).
"Being is what is nearest" (*Hum* 20), and that is why it
is so hard to think of its truth. Men find it easier to think
of that which is not so near, i.e. of beings disclosed in the
light of Being, and to forget about Being itself as "traditional metaphysics has done."

But what, then, is Being? Can it be defined in any way
other than by way of a negative theology repeating "Being

is not this, not that, it is itself"? And what is the truth of
Being forgotten by metaphysics? Heidegger answers these
questions as before: *"Die Lichtung selber aber ist das Sein"*
(*Hum* 20). The truth of Being and Being itself are the same.
Being *is* in its self disclosure as its self-disclosure. It is
what the Greeks called *aletheia,* the disclosure of Being.

This would explain why in *Being and Time* it is said
that there is Being only as long as there is disclosure, but
still the question remains: what is the relation of Being to
Dasein, the shepherd of the truth of Being, the guardian
and preserver of Being itself? Heidegger himself asks and
answers this question in *Letter on Humanism:* "But how is
Being, if one may ask this as bluntly as that, related to
ec-sistence? Being Itself is the relation insofar as It holds
ec-sistence in its existential, i.e. ecstatic essence, to Itself,
gathering it unto Itself as the abode of the truth of Being
in the midst of all that is" (*Hum* 20).

It is in the light of this definition that Heidegger now
reinterprets what he said about fall, authenticity, unauthenticity, and disclosure in *Being and Time.* "Because man, as
the ec-sistent, comes to stand in this relation as which
(relation) Being grants itself, and endures it ecstatically,
i.e. accepts it in his care, he fails, at first, to recognize what
is nearest" (ibid.). He is so occupied with and absorbed in
his daily care of beings that he forgets about "proximity
itself" and neglects the truth of Being. This oblivion is
what fall (cf. *Being and Time*) now means for Heidegger.
And, likewise, "authenticity" and "unauthenticity" in *Being
and Time* can be understood only on the basis of the
relation of Being to man. This relation being the essence
of man, authentic existence is one in which man fulfills his
essence by answering the call of Being. Unauthentic
existence is the failure to become essential, but even this
is not really man's failure, just as authenticity is not really

man's achievement. It is Being that grants or fails to grant itself authentically. The "oblivion of Being" inherent in unauthentic existence or unauthentic philosophy (Western metaphysics) is not the result of human shortcomings. This oblivion is but one of the ways in which Being discloses itself, and it has, apparently, been the fate of metaphysics that all through its history Being has been disclosing itself unessentially, leaving thought in the oblivion of the essential truth of Being.

Like fall, authenticity, and unauthenticity, language, too, obtains a new interpretation. It is no longer primarily the meaningful articulation of Being-in-the-world as disclosed by Dasein to Dasein but is the "house of Being" inhabited by man who "belongs to the truth of Being he preserves in ec-sistence" (*Hum* 22). Language, the house of Being, is erected by Being as man's abode. Its essence is to correspond with and respond to the truth of Being. Language is a *homologein*, a co-respondence to the *logos* that is, however, no longer our word but the Word. We merely "say the same" (*homologein*), i.e. say It, and thereby fulfill our essence to the extent that it lies in our power to do so. We cannot escape our fate, "for how could someone, whose essence belongs to Disclosure, ever evade the acceptance and preservation of Disclosure?" (*Vortr* 281). But our fate is not of our making, it is the Fate— *Geschick, moira,* mission, self-granting—of Being.

In all these redefinitions we find the same emphasis. It is no longer the humanity of man as ec-sistence that is essential for the definition of human existence; what must be stressed above all is the truth of Being as the proper dimension, realm, abode of the ecstatic ec-sistence of man (*Hum* 22). If readers of *Being and Time* interpreted the analysis of Dasein humanistically, i.e. as an *apotheosis* of man, and saw in Sartre's thesis, *"précisément nous sommes sur un plan où il y a seulement des hommes"* (*L'Existen-tialisme est un humanisme* 36), a radicalization of that analysis, they were altogether wrong, according to what Heidegger says now: In the spirit of *Being and Time* "one would have to say: *précisément nous sommes sur un plan où il y a principalement l'Être"* (*Hum* 22). Even this would be an inexact formulation, for Being and the "plane" where we are are one and the same. Furthermore, the French *il y a* does not render the German *es gibt* correctly. " *'Es gibt' das Sein"* means that It, i.e. Being, gives Itself, i.e. its truth, its disclosure. *"Nous sommes sur un plan où il y a l'Être"* means simply that we stand within the self-disclosure of Being. The happening of this self-disclosure is the happening, fate, mission, self-commission, self-unfolding, event, advent, and history of Being.

Heidegger's statement in *Being and Time,* " 'There is' Being only insofar as Dasein is," has been interpreted as making Being subservient to Dasein. But, in line with the preceding interpretation of *"es gibt,"* this sentence is to be understood as saying: only as long as Being discloses itself does Being 'give Itself' to man. Being entrusts itself to man only in its self-disclosure. The sentence does not say that Being is the product of man, for the *"es gibt,"* the self-disclosure of Being, is Being's own accomplishment. Far from Being being the projection of man, man is the "thrown projection" of Being, projected by Being into ec-sistence, i.e. Its self-disclosure. As the project of Being, man is the shepherd of its truth. "He acquires the essential poverty of the shepherd whose dignity consists in being called by Being itself into the preservation of its truth. This call comes as the throw that is the source of the thrownness of Dasein" (*Hum* 29). Man, ec-sisting, answers the call, "lives in the proximity of Being" and becomes "the neighbor of Being" (ibid.).

Truth and the Word

With Heidegger's descent into the "poverty of thought," there is an increasing emphasis in his works on man's possession by and ecstatic service of a Power greater than man, whose call man answers by existing. This is especially noticeable in his latest essays, written in the fifties, on the subject of language. *Toward Language* does not introduce any new topics into our discussion. Word, language, speech are but new names for *logos, physis, aletheia,* etc., the fundamental phenomenon we have been dealing with all along. The novelty of the essays lies in the strengthening of Heidegger's quasi-religious tone and ecstatic-mystical attitude toward the self-revelation of Being.

Language is still the "house of Being" (*U* 90) in these essays, but it almost seems as if it were Being's only abode, i.e. mode of disclosure. Where words are lacking, nothing is: no thing, no god, no world, no self. All is dark. There is no light, no disclosure, no Being. (*U* 176–77). Words alone lend things substance by bringing them to stand, i.e. to stand within the light where they can be what they are. The function of language is "saying" (*sagan, sagen, Sage*) and to say means literally to declare, to make clear, light, bright, shining, and apparent, "to show, to make manifest, to let something be seen and heard" (*U* 252). "Saying is by no means the temporally subsequent verbal expression of that which appears (prior to the expression); much rather, all appearing and disappearing is founded on the saying that makes apparent. It (the saying) delivers what is present into its presence and casts off what is absent into its absence." (*U* 257). Thus, "illuminating-concealing," saying, "delivers, i.e. offers, hands over, what we call world" (*U* 200).

Logos qua saying is the same as *logos* qua thinking.

What is true of thinking is true of saying too. "Thinking is
not a means for knowledge. Thinking draws furrows in the
field of Being" (*U* 173) and "they open up the field so
that it can shelter seed and growth" (*U* 252). And this is
what saying does. It promotes growth in the sense of *physis:*
unfolding into disclosure. Both thinking and saying refer
to *aletheia* and are but different names for establishing
the presence of what is present in disclosure (*U* 237). "The
essence of saying is the saying of Essence" (*U* 176), i.e. the
disclosure of Being. Therefore word, language, and speech
are essential (are what they are) only insofar as in and
through them Being comes to word (*U* 196, 201).

The ancient Greeks characterized man as the being that
is, in some manner, possessed of speech. This characterization still expresses the essence of man in Heidegger. Man
is man only insofar as he is "saying," i.e. bringing the word
into its own (into its essence: the disclosure of Being). But
this act, as we have seen in the case of "thinking," is not
man's act. Instead of saying "man speaks," it is more
accurate to say, according to Heidegger, that "language
speaks." And instead of saying that "man utters, gives
forth words," one ought to say that "the Word gives; It is
the Giver, It gives: Being. It, the Word, gives" (*U* 193)
Itself to man, and in granting Itself thus It gives man his
essence, his humanity. Man does not use language; language
uses man. The event and advent of Being in and through
language, word, and saying "puts man to use for Its own
sake" (*U* 261). This is no abuse, for only in this use can
man be essential. "Man is man only insofar as, devoted to
the call of language, he is used for language, for the speaking
of language" (*U* 196). "What is brought about (in this use),
the essence of man, is brought into its own through language
in order that it serve the essence of language . . . Such an
event comes about insofar as the essence of language . . .
uses mortal speaking . . . in order to be audible to mortal

hearing" (*U* 30). Human speech is a "co-respondence," a response to Being. "Having heard the summons" it hearkens to the command and "follows the call" (*U* 32) and thereby fulfills, i.e. brings into its essence, language, the humanity of man, and Being Itself, all three together.

In *Toward Language* Heidegger's "phenomenological hermeneutic" undergoes its third metamorphosis. Phenomenological hermeneutic in *Being and Time* meant an interpretation of Dasein's existence, i.e. understanding of Being. In consequence, the fundamental ontology of *Being and Time* turned out to be humanistic, metaphysical: a philosophical anthropology. In the later writings of Heidegger phenomenological hermeneutic became more and more historical. It was through an interpretation (*hermeneuein*) of the thought of great philosophers and poets that Heidegger attempted to show how Being manifested itself (*phainesthai, legein*) in the history of human thought. Now, in one of his last essays on language, he interprets phenomenological hermeneutic in yet another way. The term hermeneutic, he explains, stems from his study of theology, a study "without which I would never have come upon the path of thought" (*U* 96), but it is used by him in a sense divergent from the theological use. Trying to "think what is thought in Greek in an even more originally Greek sense" (*U* 134) than the Greeks were capable of, Heidegger derives *hermeneuein* from Hermes, the messenger of the gods who brings men divine tidings of their fate, and translates it as "the bringing of message and tiding" (*U* 122). Thus hermeneutic is a kind of "proffering that brings word insofar as it is able to hearken to a message" (*U* 121). It is not merely a discipline or method of thought, as it is in theology; hermeneutic is the name for the essence, existence, and humanity of man. For "man is man only insofar as he hearkens to the message" (*U* 135), he is human only insofar as he is employed for the hearing and bearing of the tiding. This employment is the essential mission of man, to which he is committed by that which, making him the bearer, commits itself to man, the messenger (*U* 136). "It is the Message itself that uses us as messengers" (*U* 155) who bear the word and endure the enormity of the task. We are but heralds declaring what is declared unto us. It might not even be right to say that the message is directed at us, principally. Speech is essentially a monologue. The mystery of language is that "It speaks, alone and lonesome, to Itself" (*U* 241).

It is in this manner that Heidegger now understands his own mission as *hermeneus:* the mission consists in "making manifest that which is Wholly Other, and is only darkly, if not confusedly, divined" (*U* 128) by man. This is what the Greek poets engaged in in the theater of Dionysus: it was in their "saying itself that the approach of the god came to pass. The saying itself made manifest what the sayers beheld (and they beheld It) because It had beforehand already cast an eye upon them" (*U* 219). If Heidegger occasionally succeeds in this mission, so that traces of that which is Wholly Other can be discerned in his writing, this is not his accomplishment; he merely finds these traces: "I merely find them, for they do not stem from me and are but seldom perceptible, like the scattered echoes of a far-away call" (*U* 131). "All I did was to follow the indefinite traces of a road; but (at least) I followed" (*U* 137). Erring on this road "through the realm of the Word" (*U* 235) is the errand of the thinker and sayer— soothsayer in the literal sense of the word. Following the "call that wakes the saying," the sayer of truth is moved by the "spirit whose gentle breath insinuates itself into the soul" (*U* 235). Like the apostles (literally: messengers), on whose heads tongues of flame descended so that they spoke "in another tongue," i.e. with the voice of the "Holy Spirit" (*U* 203), Heidegger now brings us the Word.

"Thinking is thanking" (*U* 267), a prayer as it were, whose source and destination remain a mystery.

With this last metamorphosis of the meaning of hermeneutic, Heidegger the phenomenologist has finally yielded to Heidegger the prophet, apostle, and soothsayer, the ecstatic bearer of the Word, the enthusiastic, inspired-possessed instrument, the occasional, temporary dwelling-place and fleeting incarnation of the Voice of Being.

Truth Needs Men

Heidegger's essays on language are an extreme expression of what has sometimes been called his "conversion" from Dasein to Being, i.e. his gradual shift of emphasis from a resolute authentic Dasein, whose existence is the absolute foundation of all truth, to self-granting, self-disclosing, originally essential (essence-contributing) Being as the origin of all truth. For all their radical tone, however, these essays do not represent a break within Heidegger's philosophical development; they complete rather than contradict his theories as developed since the publication of *Being and Time*. This later development has made Heidegger's thought a balanced whole: one that retains most of the results of the existentialistic analysis, but at the same time gives the existence of Dasein itself a firm foundation and thereby achieves a balance, combining two seemingly contradictory poles—existence and Being—in a dialectic of correspondence.

What must be emphasized, in view of Heidegger's relentless insistence on Being in the later essays, is that this dialectic, like all dialectic, is, in the final analysis, one of tension and opposition between two elements of equal weight. For it is true that, in the conversion, all emphasis is transferred from Dasein to Being, so that from a self-certain subject—as Dasein could still be interpreted in

Being and Time—man turns into the instrument, shepherd, and servant of Being. But it is equally true, in spite of Heidegger's occasional denial, that in this philosophy, Being, whose essence is its self-disclosure in the thought, existence, Dasein—i.e. the history—of man, is exhausted with the happening of truth in our existence, and is thus essentially dependent on the existence of man.

Being is, i.e. happens in and as, its self-revelation or history, and this history is inconceivable without the existence of the historical being: man. The history of Being is the history, i.e. process of happening, of the humanity of man; it is, as it were, a "human" history of Being. In spite of the intensity of Heidegger's "dehumanization" of thought, nothing could be more evident than the fact that, in a sense, Heidegger also succeeded in "humanizing" Being in his philosophy. No matter how much he exalts the pole opposite to Dasein in the later writings, the Word still needs speakers, Truth still needs sayers, the Message needs messengers, and Spirit its embodiments to be inspired. The finitude of man is, in the end, taken up into Being, which itself becomes finite in Heidegger, standing under the *chre* of Parmenides, i.e. needing essentially—in order to be disclosed, in order to be—the existence of man. What Heidegger quite rightly remarks of Hegel's *Phenomenology,* namely that "our being belongs to the *parousia* of the Absolute" (*Holzw* 176) and that this *parousia* is in a sense "our contribution," is literally true of his own philosophy. Here too, human Dasein essentially belongs to and is necessary for the *parousia,* i.e. the truth, self-disclosure, essence of Being.

Nietzsche's Zarathustra greeted the sun with the words: "Thou great star. What would be thy fortune if thou didst not have those for whom thou shinest? Ten years thou hast come up to my cave here: thou wouldst have become weary of thy light and of thy road without me, my eagle

and my snake" (*Also sprach Zarathustra,* 1883, no. 5).
According to Heidegger these words characterize the
history of philosophy from Plato to Nietzsche, and express
"the core of the whole of Western thought" (*WhD* 28). If
so, Heidegger's own thought is thoroughly embedded in
this history, whose unbroken tradition it continues.

Heidegger himself seems to admit this at times, and he
explains the man-relatedness of his philosophy by asserting
that all thought is essentially a kind of metaxy: thinking
that necessarily moves between the poles of Being and
man and remains entirely within their relation. "Every
philosophical, i.e. thoughtful, theory of the essence of man
is *in itself already* a theory of the Being of beings. Every
theory of Being is *in itself already* a theory of the essence
of man" (*WhD* 73–74, Heidegger's italics). "We ask about
the relation between the essence of man and the Being of
beings. But, as soon as I thoughtfully say 'the essence of
man,' I have already expressed therein the relation to Being.
In the same way, as soon as I say thoughtfully: Being of
beings, the relation to the essence of man is already named
therein. In each of the two members of the relation between
the essence of man and Being, the relation is already
included" (*WhD* 74). *"No* way of thought . . . starts with
the essence of man and goes from there over to Being, nor
does it, the other way around, start with Being and then
return to man. Much rather, every mode of thought is always
already *moving within* the whole relationship between Being
and the essence of man, or else it is no thought at all" (*WhD*
74, Heidegger's italics).

It is in this manner, as moving on this road within this
relation, that Heidegger would now have us view the whole
of his philosophy from *Being and Time* to *Toward
Language*. Regardless of which member of the relationship
—Being or man—he happened to emphasize in any one of
his writings, he would now have us give equal weight to

the other and keep it in mind so as to complete the relation. The resulting synthesis enables us to see the corresponding poles of his dialectic, and thus his philosophy as a whole, in the proper perspective.

The complementary poles of Heidegger's earlier and later thought viewed as a whole are easy to find:

Dasein is in the truth, i.e. its mode of Being is to be disclosing (Being) and to be disclosed (in its Being) to itself (*BT*). Being is in the truth because its essence is to be self-disclosing, in and through the existence of Dasein, but ultimately to Itself (later writings).

Dasein is worldly; the world, *kosmos,* belongs to it as disclosed by and to it; Dasein is Being-in-the-world (*BT* and *G*). The world (men and gods) is a grant of Being qua self-disclosure; Being is *physis,* the unfolding into the light of all that is (*Holzw, E, Vortr*).

Dasein is characterized by "thrown projection" (facticity and existentiality in *BT*). Being is the thrower that projects Dasein into its disclosure and thereby projects Itself as this disclosure in Dasein's existence (*Hum*).

Dasein's essence is to be concerned about its own Being and thus to be open toward and related to Being itself (*BT*). The essence of Being is to establish this openness and this relation; to establish itself as the relation of Being to man (*WhD, Hum*).

The essence of Dasein is to accomplish thought, i.e. to preserve the disclosure of Being. The essence of Being is to call man into thought and thereby to unfold thought as the thought of Being, i.e. the self-disclosure of Being in the thought of man.

Truth is relative to Dasein as the being that discloses (*BT*). Truth is relative, above all, to Being, since Dasein, the being that discloses, is itself relative to Being, and truth is but the self-disclosure of Being as this relation (of Being to Dasein) (*Hum*).

Dasein may be authentic in resolute existence (*BT*) and, ultimately, in essential thought, thinking of the truth of Being. Being may disclose itself essentially by granting itself fully in disclosure, or it may reveal itself in such a manner that in spite of the revelation it remains in oblivion, thus abandoning mankind in a certain historical period to unauthentic existence (e.g. Western metaphysics from Plato to Nietzsche).

The essence of Dasein as an ontological being is to be aware of the "ontological difference," the difference between beings and Being (*BT* and *G*). The essence of Being is to unfold the "ontological difference" by disclosing itself in and through beings in the essential thought (ontology) of man (*Vortr,* "Moira," pp. 244–50).

Ontology is phenomenological hermeneutic, an inquiry into Being by way of an investigation of Dasein's understanding of Being. True ontology, the *legein* of *eon emmenai,* is hermeneutic phenomenology in the sense of the Message making use of the messengers (*hermeneis*) for saying (*legein*), unfolding, and bringing to light (*phainesthai*) the phenomenon par excellence (*phainomenon to phainestaton*): Being itself.

"There is" Being only as long as truth is, i.e. as long as Dasein, the being in the truth exists (*BT*). Dasein ec-sists only as long as Being grants itself as the trust Dasein preserves by ec-sisting (*Hum*).

Dasein is the disclosure of its own Being as the "there" of Being-in-the-world (*BT*). Dasein is the "there," i.e. disclosure, of Being, the self-disclosure of Being itself.

One could go on indefinitely, enumerating the analogous meanings of terms applied to Dasein on the one hand and to Being on the other. Heidegger's "conversion" gives a key to the transformation of all of Dasein's modes of Being (*BT*) into modes of Being of Being itself (later writings), so that the corresponding poles of the relation Dasein-Being can easily be found.

More important, however, than this enumeration, is to note that besides this analogy there is a further, more genuine, correspondence between Being and Dasein that makes their relation truly dialectical. This relation is not a static, harmonious tension and opposition of polar terms, but is a real co-respondence and *dia-logos,* in which each of the corresponding relata is dynamically related to the other. Dasein is the "response" (in the co-respondence) to the call of Being: its thought is not a static vision and contemplation of independent, eternal truths, but a dynamic *legein* and *noein,* a thinking that unfolds, accepts in care, and preserves the disclosure of Being. But Being itself is not an immutable, self-contained, and self-sufficient Absolute, whose truth resides, independently of man, in the heavenly spheres *(en hyperouranio topo).* It is a genuinely dialectical Being whose Being is the dialogue, i.e. its granting itself for man's *legein* and *noein.* Although Heidegger speaks at times of the "monologue" of language discoursing "alone and lonesome, to Itself" *(U* 241), it is clear that this "monolectic" discourse takes place only dialectically, i.e. through and by means of *(dia)* the thought and language *(logos)* of man. The relation between Being and man is not a serene, abstract *theoria* but, rather, a Heracleitean *polemos:* the self-sacrificing, self-fulfilling struggle of man to become essential by being fully involved in and spending himself in the dialogue; and the self-granting, self-dispensing, and self-fulfilling fight of Being to become essential by sending forth man into *his* essence (the relation) so that Its essence (the same relation, the dialogue) may unfold. Being is not exempt from finitude and need. Its need is precisely the need of man: the relation. The history of this dialectical relationship is the process of happening Heideg-

ger tries to revive and revitalize in our "time of need." In
this effort he revives and literally sets in motion not only
all that is (all beings) but Being itself. In a Heracleitean-
Hegelian manner, he thinks of all that is as Becoming, and
of Being itself as History: the history of its truth or self-
disclosure in and through human existence.

Waiting for Truth

Heidegger's philosophy, viewed in this manner as a balanced
whole (of early and late writings) presenting a dialectic of
correspondence (of man and Being), has real philosophical
merit. It is a pity, therefore, that, in Heidegger's last writings,
the balance of this whole becomes precarious and the
dialectic of correspondence between man and Being loses
most of its vitality.

In *Gelassenheit* and *Nothing Is without Ground,* Heidegger is still pursuing his aim of correcting the overemphasis
on Dasein (in *BT*) by thinking of Being itself rather than
of Dasein, and thereby giving Dasein the firm foundation
it lacked in the self-founding efforts of the existentialistic
analysis. But his last attempts to introduce balance into
his writings prove to be too much of a good thing: they
overcompensate for the shortcomings of *Being and Time*
with the effect that, in the end, *Gelassenheit* and *Nothing
Is without Ground* do not complement but rather flatly
contradict the results of the existentialistic analysis, and
Heidegger's thought (from *BT* to *SG*) can no longer be
viewed as one internally consistent balanced whole.

Another unfortunate result of Heidegger's overemphasis
on Being is that the dialectic of correspondence, between
man and Being, while still retained, becomes extremely
vague. Its movement is slowed, its outlines are blurred, and
its structure becomes so indefinite that it is increasingly

hard to make out what, if anything, is still taking place in the dialogue of Being and man.

To be sure, prophetic ecstasy, hermeneutic enthusiasm, and inspired possession had little enough to do with wild frenzy and orgiastic abandon even in *Toward Language*. Far from being violent, our devotion to and service of Being and Truth was more like a state of bright, clear, calm, peaceful repose, transfused, at times at least, with an almost unobscured, translucent light. But now Heidegger ceases even to invoke Being for inspiration; he merely waits for Truth in a state of serene *Gelassenheit*.

In its original use, by the German mystics, *Gelassenheit* denoted the attitude and state of mind of a man who had resigned his own will, taken leave of himself and the world, and, relinquishing all that is earthly, had devoted, entrusted, and abandoned himself totally to God. The word had the connotation of a double movement: away from oneself and the world, and to God. In spite of Heidegger's reluctance to speak of God—"we come too late for the gods and too early for Being" (*ED* 7)—his use of the word carries the same overtones and refers to a relationship structurally the same as mystic *Gelassenheit*.

In an address entitled *"Gelassenheit"* (delivered in 1955), Heidegger repeats, by way of introducing his subject, his often pronounced objections to scientific-technological thinking. Such thought, he claims, is in fact but a flight from essential thought, an "attack on the life and essence of man" (*Gel* 22), a violation of man and his world that threatens the very foundations of human existence. To escape the dire consequences of scientific thinking man must change his ways. He need not give up the benefits and advantages of modern technology, but he must take a different attitude toward them. He may use them but at the same time beware of being used by them. Man may use things, but at the same time he should "let them rest in themselves as something that is not our most inward and proper concern" (*Gel* 24), "let them rest in themselves as things that are nothing absolute but themselves depend on something higher" (*Gel* 25). This attitude of letting things be, letting them go in order that we may be touched by something higher that is not itself a thing, is what Heidegger calls "*Gelassenheit* toward things." *Gelassenheit* to things is, at the same time an "openness for the Mystery" (*Gel* 26). In the midst of a world in which the very foundations of our existence are threatened, *Gelassenheit* to things and openness for the Mystery "promise us a new ground and foundation on which . . . we can stand and endure" (*Gel* 26).

What this new ground is is, of course, rather hard to say. As usual Heidegger finds it easier to approach the subject negatively, and so he begins his "Discussion of *Gelassenheit*" (*Gel* 29–73) by characterizing *Gelassenheit* as a kind of "nay-saying to willing" (*Gel* 33), a non-willing or "giving up of willing," a letting go of willing that lets itself in for, lets itself into, an entirely different realm of Being. "I will not to will' (*Gel* 32), Heidegger exclaims, and at the same time protests that *Gelassenheit* is not a state of passive resignation. On the contrary, it is a "higher kind of action that is, however, no activity" (*Gel* 35). It is, perhaps, best described as "nothing but waiting" (*Gel* 37).

But waiting for what? This cannot be specified, for as soon as we re-present and imagine—form an image of— what we are waiting for we sink back into the subject-object relationship which reduces everything to a thing, to an object whose objectivity is projected in the subject's projection of image-making horizons. And it is precisely this subjective-objective approach that we are supposed to transcend in *Gelassenheit*. The best one can do, therefore, is to "leave open what we are waiting for" (*Gel* 44). In this manner "the waiting lets itself in on what is Open" (*Gel* 44) without attempting to bring about, and thereby violating, Its

openness. The region we enter in waiting is open of Itself,
it is "the Overt in itself" (*Gel* 41), it is a "Region through
whose magic all that belongs to It returns to where it rests"
(*Gel* 40). It is an unnameable, yet not nameless region
(*Gel* 48), approachable only in a nonobjective, nonrepre-
senting, nonimagining, nontranscendental-horizon-making
approach. This is to say we do not approach it at all; rather,
It approaches us when we wait. Our waiting, our *Gelassenheit,* is Its gift, not our doing; we can remain wide-awake
for such waiting but never awaken it in ourselves on our
own. *"Gelassenheit* comes to us from the Region because it
consists in man's remaining open (*gelassen*) to the Region
by virtue of It. Man is in his essence left to, let into (*gelassen*)
the Region insofar as he originally belongs to It. He belongs
to It insofar as he is originally fit for the Region [*ge-eignet:*
out-fitted for, made appropriate to, and a property of the
Region] by the Region Itself" (*Gel* 51).

Gelassenheit, man's relation to the Region, is neither
an ontic nor an ontological relationship. It is not ontic
for it is far removed from any preoccupation with things
qua things, and it is not ontological because it surpasses
all transcendental imagining and representing, our ontological horizon-projecting that reduces things to objective
entities. In *Gelassenheit* it is no longer man that conditions
the conditioned (*be-dingt das Ding*) and thus lets it be; for
the first time we really let things be, i.e. leave them inviolate,
untouched by our projecting: it is the Region that now "lets
the thing in itself abide as the thing" (*Gel* 56). This is the
outcome of *Gelassenheit*. By "opening ourselves to what is
Open" (*Gel* 61) we are literally dis-closed to (*ent-schlossen,*
open for) Disclosure, the ever-abiding Truth.

This new *Ent-schlossenheit,* i.e. *Gelassenheit* to things
and openness to the Mystery, now replaces *Entschlossenheit*—the authentic resolve of *Being and Time*—as the
noblest possible attitude or act on the part of man. Nobility

means "to have origin" and "to abide at the source of one's
essence" (*Gel* 62), and man's origin, the source of his
essence, is the Region, so that it is essential—and therefore
noble—for him to abide in this Region by being open to It.
Should man be capable of such nobility—"in the manner
of waiting . . . provided that this (waiting) is *gelassen* . . .
and the essence of man remains proper to . . . [the Region]
whence we are called"—there is a hope that "wonder might
open what is Closed" (*Gel* 73).

It is, perhaps, hardly surprising that the "Discussion of
Gelassenheit" closes on this note of vague promise of a
shadowy hope, without clarifying what exactly *Gelassenheit*
involves on our part, let alone what exactly we are involved
with in *Gelassenheit*. What is surprising is, rather, that in
spite of his insistence on the transcendent nature of his
subject Heidegger attempts to clarify it, and, having failed
once, returns to the subject again in *Nothing Is without
Ground*.[14] Although this work makes no explicit mention
of *Gelassenheit*, it deals with the same problem, and, while
it is not much more successful in clarifying the problem
than *Gelassenheit* is, it is instructive to read for it throws
some further light on Heidegger's last stand with respect to
Being and truth.

Nothing Is without Ground is an investigation of the
proposition that has come to be known philosophically as
the *principium rationis sufficientis,* the principle of sufficient
reason. This principle is formulated variously as *nihil sine
ratio, nichts ist ohne Grund,* nothing is without reason.
Whatever its formulation, Heidegger claims, its truth seems
self-evident. It takes no effort on our part to see that nothing
is or can be without any reason or ground.

Why is it, Heidegger asks at the beginning of his

14. Although *SG* (1957) was published prior to *Gel* (1959), the
latter was written, according to Heidegger, in 1944–45.

investigation, that the principle seems so easy for us to understand? For no other reason, he answers, than that the principle itself originates in the human understanding. Our understanding always searches for grounds and justifications; even its own judgments must be well-grounded and justified to be understandable. Our reason always demands reasons—and reasons for these reasons—and will not accept any statement as reasonable unless it rests on rational grounds. The principle of sufficient reason is a fundamental principle simply because it is based on human reason as its foundation. "Whether we know it or not, whether we pay special attention to what we know or not, our dwelling on earth, our way through the world is always on the way to grounds and to the Ground. Whatever we encounter we find a ground for; often we do this quite superficially, at times we go deeper, and seldom enough dare we approach right to the brink of the abysses of thought" (*SG* 26). Still, the principle rules all our reasoning: it rules because it originates in our reason and is its rule.

Now what does the principle mean? In its usual, immediately understandable form, the principle states: nothing *is* without reason or ground. This means: nothing can be, nothing can be regarded as a being, unless it is supported by reasons, rests on grounds, and is rationally justified in being what it is. The Being of any being depends on its having reasons, grounds, justifications for its being such and such. To be means to have sufficient reason. Being and sufficient ground are the same.

It is, of course, easy to see what this reason or ground, wherein the Being of a being consists, must satisfy in order to be acceptable and sufficient. The reasons for the Being of any being must be sufficient to human reason, they must satisfy the human understanding. And they will be satisfactory only if they are given in terms understandable to the understanding, i.e. in the terms *of,* in the terms inherent in, our understanding. Sufficient reasons mean: reasons sufficient to the demands of reason, and that means reasons given within the framework projected by reason in its demand for reasons. To qualify as grounds (of the Being of a being) grounds must accord with and conform to the conditions of human cognition. The principle is justly called the *principium reddendae rationis,* because in giving reasons we merely give them, hand them back (*reddere*) to where all such reasons come from: the reason, understanding, cognition of man.

This being so, all reasons and grounds given in our justification of and accounting for the Being of any being are relative to the *ratio,* i.e. the subjectivity, of the subject. Being and truth degenerate into objectivity and objective disclosure for and by the subject. The principle of sufficient reason, in its usual, understandable form, is not only grounded in human reason as its foundation: It makes reason, the subjectivity of the subject, the ultimate ground and foundation of all truth and Being.

Now we have seen, especially in Chapter 2, that the *principium rationis,* in this interpretation and with these consequences, is highly objectionable to Heidegger. Ever since the thirties, he criticized the whole of Western metaphysics for its alleged subjectivism and humanism, i.e. precisely because it stood under the rule of the principle of sufficient reason in the form just discussed, even though this principle was not explicitly formulated until Leibniz. It was this rule that made Western philosophy—culminating in modern scientific technology—an attack on the world and a violation of the essence of man, and marked the oblivion of truth and Being in which traditional philosophy has remained, according to Heidegger, up to our days. This approach to the world is certainly the direct opposite of what Heidegger now counsels us to adopt as the only way to escape an unessential existence: *Gelassenheit* to things and openness to the Mystery.

The question is, do we have to disregard, or even deny and discard the principle of sufficient reason, this highest and mightiest principle of human reason, in order to effect the desired transformation of both philosophy and human existence? No, Heidegger answers, we only have to understand the principle differently. We do not have to give up thought, but we have to change—radically—our modes of thinking. And we can begin to do this by rethinking the sentence we have been dealing with: Nothing is without ground.

In the sense in which we understood this principle, it meant: nothing is without reason, nothing is without a "because" that answers the "why?" of reason in the terms in which this "why?" is projected by reason. It meant: "Nothing is without why" (*SG* 68). But it was no lesser man than Angelus Silesius, the seventeenth-century mystic and philosopher, who once declared: "The rose is without why." Did Angelus Silesius dare to contradict the principle of sufficient reason?

Angelus Silesius' poem is entitled "Without Why."[15] It says:

The rose is without why; it blooms because it blooms,
It cares not for itself, asks not if it's seen.

What does the poem mean?

Angelus Silesius' rose, Heidegger explains, "obviously stands for all that blooms, for all growing things, for all growth" (*SG* 69). It is blooming as "pure unfolding out of itself, pure shining" (*SG* 101), appearing and Being, that is "without why." But how can such unfolding and bloom-

15. Angelus Silesius, *Der Cherubinische Wandersmann* (1657), book 1, no. 289.

ing be without *why* and yet bloom *because* it blooms? Are
not *why* and *because* so inseparably connected that Angelus
Silesius' line becomes self-contradictory? Not according to
Heidegger's interpretation: "The why seeks the ground"
(*SG* 70), asks for grounds, while the because refers (us) to
the ground, and "proffers the ground" (*SG* 70). And the
ground it proffers is by no means the same as the one the
why seeks, as the second line of the poem clearly shows:

It cares not for itself, asks not if it's seen.

"The rose is rose without having to be concerned with
itself. It does not need . . . to care for itself. Caring for
itself and, consequently, for all that belongs to it by virtue
of determining it, i.e. giving it ground, does not belong to
the manner in which the rose is" (*SG* 71). Unlike man who
always seeks determining grounds for all, who is always
concerned with himself and all that belongs to him, the
rose blooms unconcerned. It blooms because it blooms:
blooming, the pure unfolding out of itself, "happens to the
rose" (*SG* 71), the rose is in-folded in this unfolding without
any concern for something else that could be regarded as
a cause and condition of possibility of its blooming. The
rose neither seeks nor gives reasons (*reddit rationem*), and
thus the *principium reddendae rationis* does not apply to
it in the sense in which it was discussed above. This principle
is true "*of* the rose but not *for* the rose; of the rose insofar
as it is an object of our representation, not for the rose
insofar as it stands in itself, insofar as it is simply rose"
(*SG* 73).

Now Angelus Silesius is not content, according to Heidegger, with merely pointing out the difference between
the modes of Being of man and rose. "The unuttered point
of the poem—and this is what is all important—is that in
the most hidden recesses of his Being man *is* truly only
when in his own way he is as the rose—without why"

(*SG* 73). To be what we essentially are we have to become like the rose: we have to live without care and concern, without seeking, questioning, and demanding grounds. This does not mean that man's life has to become groundless and ungrounded. For Angelus Silesius says, "The rose blooms *because* it blooms," i.e. in some manner the rose does proffer and bring with itself its own ground. What we have to keep in mind here is simply the difference in the relations to ground implied by the "why" and the "because." With the "why?" we attack the world and demand justification—ground—for its Being. "In the 'why' we posit the ground to give us account and answer" (*SG* 78). But our attitude is quite different when, instead of demanding grounds, we humbly accept the ground proffered in the "because": "In the 'because' we yield ourselves to the grounded thing; we relinquish the thing to itself and to the manner in which the Ground, in grounding it, simply lets the thing be what it is" (*SG* 78).

This is our task if we want to be what we truly are: we have to live—like the rose—without why so that we can accept—and thus rest on, be grounded in—the Ground that proffers Itself with the "because," i.e. with the simple self-unfolding of what unfolds itself on its own. If we live *gelassen* to things—without why, without a ground-laying attack on the world—and open for the Mystery, the Mystery, the Ground, will yield Itself to us because we have yielded—delivered ourselves—to It.

"The rose blooms because it blooms." In view of the preceding it is no longer possible to translate Angelus Silesius in this manner. "Because" has too strong a connotation of "causes," the kind of grounds that the "why?" seeks and provides. To be true to the spirit of the poem we must modify the translation. The German *"weil"* means, here, "while," "during," and "to while means: to endure, to remain still, to abide in oneself and hold still, i.e. in peace" (*SG* 207). "To while, to endure, to abide forever is, however, the old sense of the word: to be" (*SG* 207–08). The Ground that is proffered in the simple unfolding of the rose, the Ground we accept and rest on when we abandon all whys and abandon ourselves to the Ground, is simply: Being. "Being and Ground are the same" (*SG* 43, 94, 129, 185).

This Ground is no longer a cause, not even a first or last cause, and least of all its own cause, a *causa sui*. It is not any kind of sufficient ground that would answer the question "why?". Indeed, this Ground is not an answer to anything. But this is precisely Heidegger's point, that instead of seeking for answers we should be more prepared to accept what is given to us when we least expect it, when we only wait—*gelassen* and open to the Mystery.

Goethe saw the utter vanity of our ground-laying attack on the world:

Wie? Wann? und Wo?—Die Goetter bleiben stumm!
Du halte dich ans Weil und frage nicht Warum?[16]

And so did Meister Eckhart, whose work, according to Heidegger, manifests what "extreme keenness and depth of thought belong to all genuine and great mysticism" (*SG* 71). In a sermon entitled "The Innermost Ground" Meister Eckhart writes:

Should someone keep asking Life, for a thousand years: Why doest thou live? if it should answer it would not speak otherwise than: I live because I live. And this is so because Life lives out of its own ground and springs forth out of its own: therefore it lives without why, simply living Itself.

The question "why?" is ultimately self-defeating. The answers human reason provides are an endless chain of

16. Goethe, *Spruchsammlung aus dem Jahre 1815,* quoted by Heidegger (*SG* 206 ff.).

contingent reasons without a last link, a chain that is not
fastened to any unshakable ground. In trying to find a
ground for himself by questioning, man only takes back the
ground he projects, i.e. he "hands back" (*reddere*) grounds
(*rationes*) to where they spring from, his own *ratio,* which
they can thus never securely justify and support as ground.
And Life—Being, *physis,* the gods, whatever name we may
choose to call It—gives no answers. It remains mute. It
simply is.

In the face of such silence we must abandon the life of
reason and human understanding, the life of care and
concern, of seeking and questioning "why?". We must abandon ourselves totally, with the whole of our Being, to Being,
the Mystery, the self-granting Ground. This abandon—
Gelassenheit—is man's only remaining hope for salvation.

But what saves us in this salvation? What is this new
Ground on which man has to rest in order to escape a
groundless, foundering existence? Heidegger's answer is
obscure enough to do justice to his subject matter.

The Ground is Itself measureless and groundless. It
cannot be measured in terms of our measure, it cannot be
sounded by our understanding, it cannot be given foundation by our rational ground-laying. The Ground has no
ground. "Being qua Being remains ground-less . . . Being
[is]: the Abyss [*Ab-grund*]" (*SG* 185). Being is the Abyss
whose dreaded brink we approach when we will not to will,
it is the Abyss into which we leap in essential thought. This
leap of thought does not hurl us into a measureless void.
On the contrary, through the leap thought begins to "correspond to Being qua Being, i.e. to the truth of Being" (*SG*
185). "Through this leap thought arrives in the wide (open
regions) of the play on which our human essence is staked.
Only insofar as man is brought into this play and is at stake
in the play can he truly play and remain in the play" (*SG*
186).

Angelus Silesius called man "the lyre-play of God."[17]
But Heidegger finds Heracleitus even more expressive of
his own meaning. For Heracleitus characterized *aion*
(eternity, which is, for Heidegger, the same as World-time,
the mission, self-commission of Being) as a "child that
plays" (fr. 52). In Heidegger too, Being is a Play, the
Ground-play, the Ground-giver giving Itself in play.

> It plays, because it plays.

> The "because" submerges in the game. The game is with-
> out "why." It plays while it plays. It remains only play:
> the highest and deepest.

> But this "only" is All, the One, the Only One.

> Nothing *is* without *Ground*. Being and Ground: the same.
> Being as Ground-giving has no ground, as Abyss it plays
> the game which as Fate deals us Being and Ground.

> The question remains whether and in what manner . . . we
> play along and abandon ourselves to the game (*SG* 188).

These lines, the closing lines of Heidegger's lecture-
course are Heidegger's last hint in the direction of his
mysterious Ground. That they are no more than a hint is
no wonder. As all mystics know and as Heidegger himself
insists, the Ground is unutterable, ineffable, indescribable;
it is beyond all human reasoning and understanding. It is
transcendent par excellence; it is Transcendence itself.

Obscure as Heidegger's hint may be, it makes one thing
abundantly clear: what was once called authentic existence
—existence as a concern for and understanding of Being,
an ultimately self-directed concern, a restless seeking and
questioning of one's own ground—will no longer do. Since

17. *Der Cherubinische Wandersmann,* book 5, no. 366.

ever-questioning Dasein only encounters the silence of the gods, since the world only reflects the questioner's vacant stare, since Being gives no answers but only is, i.e. endures and abides, man too has to endure in the face of such ultimate, un-grounded silence. Abandoning his "existential" nature he has to abandon himself to the Ground, leap into the Abyss, and stake himself on the Play of Being in which Truth discloses Itself—now that we no longer search but only wait—as Mystery.

No matter how much the character of Dasein and its role in the disclosure of Being have changed here, however, Dasein and Being still belong together even in Heidegger's last, most prophetic and mystical writings.

In *Identity and Difference,* an address delivered a year after Heidegger gave his lectures on *Nothing Is without Ground,* Heidegger writes: "There prevails in man a belonging to Being, which belonging (*Gehoeren*) hearkens to (*hoert*) Being because it is assigned to It. And what about Being? Let us think of Being in its original sense as Presence. Being is present to man neither just by the way nor as an exception. Being is and abides only as long as it affects man through its claim. For it is only man who, in his openness to Being, lets It arrive as Presence. Such Presence needs and uses[18] the openness of a clearing and remains, therefore, through this need and use, assigned to man. This does not at all mean that Being is first posited by man and is posited only through man. On the contrary, it becomes clear: man and Being are assigned to each other" (*Id* 22–23). Being human, we are assigned to, delivered over to, imbedded in, and "let into the belonging to Being. But Being itself belongs to us; for only in our keep can it be as Being, i.e. Presence" (*Id* 24). It is only through the Event (*Ereignis:* the disclosure of truth in the oc-currence—

---

18. Double translation of *"braucht"*.

literally coming together—of man and Being) that "man and Being attain to each other in their essence, attain their essence" (*Id* 30). "The Event delivers man and Being into their essential togetherness" (*Id* 31).

While Plato left open the question to what extent our participation in, partaking of, and assimilation to what is essential is essential to It—the Ideas, the Good, God—Heidegger's new *methexis* and *homoiosis* clearly involve an inseparable correspondence between man and Being. This correspondence, the mutual E-vent, Ad-vent, and Oc-currence—coming out, coming together and coming to be—of man and Being, is *aletheia,* disclosure, the happening of truth, and truth is not just an added, accidental trait of Being, even in *Nothing Is without Ground:* Being is not first "there, and then has the additional property of disclosing itself, but self-disclosure belongs to what is Being's own. Being has its own in self-disclosure . . . self-disclosure belongs to the essence of Being . . . to that wherein Being preserves its essence as its own" (*SG* 120–21). "Strictly speaking, we must say: Being belongs to . . . Self-disclosure" (*SG* 121). And even now, in Heidegger's latest writings, the sentence pronounced in *Being and Time* holds true: there is truth only as long as Dasein is. There can be no Disclosure without man's dis-closure (*Ent-schlossenheit*) to It.

Heidegger's attitude toward the role of man in the disclosure of Being is most ambiguous in his "Discussion of *Gelassenheit.*" But even here this role seems to be an indispensable one, one without which the Play itself could not take place. As one of Heidegger's interlocutors in the discussion puts it: "Obviously the essence of man is assigned and abandoned to the Region for the simple reason that this essence belongs to the Region so essentially that without man this (the Region) could not be as it is" (*Gel* 64). Substituting truth—the essence of the Region—for Region, he repeats: "Man is assigned to Truth because Truth needs man. But is it not the distinguishing character of Truth, and especially with respect to its relation to man, that it is what it is independently of man?" (*Gel* 65). Heidegger answers: "The essence of man is assigned and abandoned (*gelassen*) to the Region and is thus used by the Region for the sole reason that man on his own has no power over Truth and this [i.e. Truth] remains independent of him. Truth can be independent of man only because the essence of man as *Gelassenheit* to the Region is used by the Region . . . Truth's independence *of* man is nonetheless manifestly a relation *to* man" (*Gel* 65–66, Heidegger's italics). Ambiguous as this answer is, it seems to indicate that Truth is independent of man only in the sense that man on his own has no arbitrary power over Truth, that it is not up to man's decision and wilful act whether or not Truth is. For man is essentially—by virtue of his essence and by virtue of the essence of Truth—in the Truth, he is used for its disclosure whether he will or not. Thus Truth is not subject to man's whim. Nevertheless, Truth can *be* only by virtue of the fact that it always—in accordance with its own essence—uses man for the preservation of its own essence: disclosure. Man is, in short, so essentially imbedded, implicated, literally infolded in the essence of Truth, that neither man nor Truth can be without and outside their relation.

Therefore, "the mission (*Geschick*) of Being remains, in itself, the history of the being (*Wesensgeschichte*) of Western man, insofar as historical man is used in the constructive dwelling within the disclosure of Being" (*SG* 157). "For the mission of Being (*das Geschick des Seins*) is not only no process that goes on in itself, it is also nothing that confronts us, rather it is Fate (*das Geschick*) itself *as* the confrontation of Being and the being of man" (*SG* 158, Heidegger's italics).

Truth still needs man and man still needs Truth, though it is, perhaps, increasingly more difficult to say why. But this why is not a question that Heidegger encourages us to ask. In *Gelassenheit* and *Nothing Is without Ground* the fate of Being and man has become so much of a Mystery that those who want to follow Heidegger on his path can no longer ask questions. They have to abandon philosophy as reflective, self-reflective thought altogether, and find consolation and reassurance in mystical poetry and faith.

4.

BEYOND PHILOSOPHY

Beyond Metaphysics

Three decades have passed since Heidegger's much publicized conversion of thought from Dasein to Being. In these three decades Heidegger has published more than a score of writings designed to turn philosophy into a new direction by overcoming metaphysics, humanism, subjectivism, and nihilism. Have they succeeded in accomplishing this aim, and, if so, what are the results of this accomplishment for philosophy?

To answer these questions we have to deal with the three stages of Heidegger's hermeneutic separately.

Phenomenological hermeneutic as conceived and executed in *Being and Time* was clearly metaphysical.[1] As fundamental ontology it was a clarification of *man's* understanding of Being and thus remained humanistic, subjectivistic, relativistic, and nihilistic in the sense in which Heidegger now uses these terms. He saw this himself and

1. See Chapter 2, *"Being and Time* as Metaphysics."

this is what made him abandon the existentialistic analysis and search for a new approach to Being.

The second stage of Heidegger's hermeneutic seems less metaphysical at first sight. For here, in a series of writings from *Of the Essence of Truth* to *Thought,* he makes a determined attempt to define man and beings on the basis of a definition of Being, rather than vice versa, and to lay all emphasis, in the relation between man and Being, on Being rather than man. Thus in their explicit intention at least, these writings are less humanistic and subjectivistic than *Being and Time.* Unfortunately, this intention is easier to state than to fulfill.

To begin with, in spite of all verbal emphasis on Being rather than man, Being remains man-related and man-bound in all these writings. For all its supposed primacy in the relation (of man and Being), its disclosure is inevitably tied up with Dasein's self- and world-disclosure, so that truth and Being still could not be but for the existence of man.[2] Since from the point of view of Being itself (if one could ever adopt such a point of view) it might be hard to see why Being as such should be so utterly dependent for its being on the existence of the particular being we happen to be ourselves,[3] it is hard to avoid the impression that Heidegger's insistence on this dependence is little more than an all too human pretension. This pretension is, to be sure, quite understandable from the point of view of man, but, precisely because it is, it is a humanistic pretension, a claim imbued with the spirit of humanism: man's preoccupation with his own Being, and the resulting interpretation of Being itself on the basis of an all too human concern with one's own existence.

It is questionable furthermore, whether Heidegger's

2. See in Chapter 3, "Truth Needs Men."
3. It is not, e.g., in Christianity, which attempts to take a similar point of view.

method in these writings is much less humanistic than it was in *Being and Time*. In *Being and Time* "phenomenological hermeneutic" aimed at a disclosure of Being through a clarification of Dasein's understanding of Being. This method, leading to a humanistic and subjectivistic disclosure, has been discarded in favor of one that interprets (*hermeneuei*) another type of phenomenon: not Dasein's everyday world-disclosure but the rare, and therefore hopefully more essential, disclosure of Being that takes place in the thought of great historical poets and philosophers. But what guarantees that Being reveal itself in the history of human thought more originally and less distorted by *human* vision than in the unsophisticated disclosures of our everyday lives? Are not exceptional human beings, especially in their moments of heightened existence and seemingly more than human inspiration, even more liable to impose their humanity on Being, and thereby prejudice its pristine disclosure, than the unself-conscious multitude that lives without any obvious concern for Being as such? However one might be inclined to answer this question, Heidegger's great shortcoming is that he fails to provide, at this stage, any philosophical criteria whereby the matter could be decided.

The criterion that was implicit in *Being and Time*—the disclosure of Being-in-the-world—has been discarded as metaphysical and humanistic. But the history of thought, to which Heidegger now turns, is, as such, equally unacceptable to him as a criterion. The fact that the poets and philosophers he deals with are, for the most part, great figures in the history of human thought is irrelevant for Heidegger, since, unlike Hegel, he does not recognize history and tradition as valid criteria of truth. On the contrary, he rejects most of traditional philosophy as humanistic, and selects a few figures only as possessors of —or, as he puts it, possessed by—a more essential vision.

The basis of this selection, however, remains utterly obscure. It is not traditional philosophy, for this he rejects, and it cannot be any reference to everyday experience, for this would represent a return to the method of *Being and Time,* which he discarded. The only ground that remains for the selection—as well as the often extraordinary interpretation —of these works is Heidegger's own judgment based on unrevealed criteria. What Heidegger attempts at this stage is very close in method to biblical hermeneutic; only, lacking the traditional authority of the Bible, and even that of the history of philosophy, these works have to be accepted as the final authority, and Heidegger's interpretations as the authoritative ones, on Heidegger's own unsupported, and in its source unrevealed, authority.

Heidegger is well aware of the fact that any justification of his choice of works and of his interpretations by way of an appeal either to philosophical tradition or to rational reflection on everyday experience would only make his thought liable to his own charges of humanism. To escape from this philosophical embarrassment, he takes the only logical step that is still open to him: he adopts the stance of a prophet and lays claim to mystic insight and inspiration as the sole support of his dictates. Thus begins the third and final stage of his hermeneutic.

Heidegger's position as a prophet or mystic, speaking on behalf of Being, is, of course, an impregnable methodological position. The only ground on which a philosophical discussion with him would still be possible—rational reflection—he rejects as humanistic and therefore invalid, and, barring rival inspiration one can hardly dispute Heidegger's own, while, claiming such, one already concedes to him the possible authority, though not necessarily the content, of his own inspiration. And once one accepts his claim, his method becomes eo ipso unhumanistic, for the claim is precisely that this disclosure of Being is not

Heidegger's own, not an insight of man, but the result of a more than human inspiration. The argument is, of course, circular, but as such has the merit of being a closed circle that offers philosophy no point whereby to enter it. Not that philosophy has to enter the circle to refute Heidegger's argument. It is quite enough for philosophy to point out that even a nonhuman disclosure requires a human interpreter translating it into a human language rooted in and clarifying human experience before it becomes meaningful for—and thus a disclosure to—human beings.

The third stage of Heidegger's hermeneutic amply demonstrates this fact. For if Heidegger claims to speak here with a more than human—and therefore nonhumanistic—tongue, what he says is in effect almost less than human—almost completely devoid of human insight—and therefore nonhumanistic. In his attempt to make visible what is Wholly Other, and to make us enter into an entirely different dimension, Heidegger engages in a kind of negative theology and mysticism: he gives forth sibylline utterances whose only concrete content is the rejection of all human experience and insight. This is not a sudden development, for already in his second hermeneutic period Heidegger's descent into the poverty of thought was accompanied by a gradual elimination of concrete significance and existential import from his thought. But this process is now completed: Insisting on the ineffability of his ultimate Ground, the incomprehensibility of the Play of Being, and the total otherness of his Region of disclosure, Heidegger has succeeded in overcoming humanistic metaphysics. But he did so at the price of relinquishing all philosophically articulate and articulable meaning.

In his *Letter on Humanism* Heidegger had warned: "Thought does not overcome metaphysics when it transcends . . . it by ascending even higher" (*Hum* 37); on the contrary, thought would have to descend "into the poverty

of the ec-sistence of the *homo humanus*" (ibid.). But, in
the end, he has done the opposite. In his last writings
Heidegger ascended so high above human existence that,
in contrast to the barren region wherein he is now wont
to dwell, the existence of man, for all its poverty, still
seems incomparably rich in meaning. Only this meaning
is human meaning and as such has to be left behind. And so
has philosophy.

In spite of Heidegger's claim that his thinking is neither
theistic nor atheistic (*Hum* 37), he has overcome humanistic
metaphysics—as well as philosophy—only by becoming a
mystic poet and godless theologian. To be sure, his faith
has no articulate creed (but this is not necessary for
mysticism either) and no God or gods (as some religions
do not either). But, for all that, the relationship between
Being and man that now occupies his thought bears closest
resemblance to the God-man relationship that is the subject
of theology; the language he now uses is most analogous
in its structure to theological language; and his ambiguous
passion for Being is most like faith's passion for God.
Negative theology has done for a long time what Heidegger
now attempts to do, and his call out of the world (of
everyday existence, of rational questioning "why?") into
another realm is a commonplace to all mysticism and
religion. It has been pointed out (e.g. by Loewith) that
Heidegger's latest teaching—or preaching—will be most
comprehensible, if one can still speak of comprehension
in this connection, to theologians and to men of faith, and
the justice of this observation is shown by contemporary
Protestant theologians' lively interest in, and serious efforts
to come to terms with, Heidegger's thought. That this
should be so is hardly surprising; both Heidegger's method
and his message are prophetic-kerygmatic: he is publicly
announcing the coming of an unknown-unknowable Being,
and trying to prepare man for Its advent.

During his conversion of thought from Dasein to Being, Heidegger repeatedly stated that to overcome metaphysics meant not to destroy it but simply to reveal its nature: to show that it was a humanistic, subjectivistic, and nihilistic approach to Being which, oblivious of Being as such, had its limits and could not therefore be regarded as the only humanly possible approach, and to show, furthermore, that "the essential possibilities of metaphysics have been exhausted" (*N* I, 201). Thus metaphysics could not be perfected and need not be brought to an end by Heidegger; it had already been perfected and brought to an end by the work of metaphysicians, from Plato to Nietzsche, who exhausted its possibilities by realizing them all.

Paradoxically, Heidegger has fulfilled his intention of overcoming metaphysics in this manner, but his doing so does not always do him credit. For while in the first two stages of his hermeneutic he showed that the essential possibilities of metaphysics have been exhausted mainly by following—willingly or unwillingly—in the footsteps of traditional metaphysicians, the last stage of his hermeneutic has a negative rather than positive philosophical significance: it shows the limits of humanistic metaphysics most clearly by overstepping them and entering into something else, and it shows that the essential possibilities of metaphysics have been exhausted by its having to abandon philosophy in order to avoid metaphysics.

I have tried, in the course of the preceding exposition of Heidegger's philosophy, to point to some of the historical sources and ingredients of Heidegger's thought, and it is sufficient merely to summarize them here.

In the first stage of his hermeneutic—*Being and Time*—Heidegger adopts Platonic teleology in the sense of a concern for one's own good and end (ones' own Being) and for the Good (Being as such) as the essence of human rationality (existence, in Heidegger). He revives Kant's transcendental philosophy and describes the structure of phenomenal experience (Being-in-the-world) on the basis of the transcendence (existential projection) of Dasein. He successfully combines these two elements in a Platonic modification of the Kantian critique, showing Dasein's world-projection to be teleological, i.e. rooted in and expressive of Dasein's concern for its own Being and for Being as such.

In the second stage—*Of the Essence of Truth* to *Thought* —this scheme acquires more and more Hegelian overtones. Heidegger elaborates a quasi-Hegelian dialectic of correspondence between Dasein and Being, and Dasein's world-projection becomes the answer to the self-projection of Being as well as the means of the self-unfolding of this new Absolute.

Even the last stage of Heidegger's thought, which transcends philosophy, contains nothing essentially new in the history of thought. Whether we consider it a return to the sources of Hegel's dialectic—Christianity, mysticism, and early Greek philosophy—a rethinking of Parmenides' poem on the One, or merely the emotional elaboration of a Kantian Transcendental Idea, Heidegger's thought has traditional philosophical and, at its extreme, nonphilosophical precedents. This does not mean, of course, that it is therefore less valuable. On the contrary, Heidegger must be given a great deal of credit for reviving and revitalizing traditional philosophical, or nonphilosophical, problems and expressing them in a contemporary idiom. But one cannot give him credit for this and at the same time agree with his contention of opening up altogether new paths for philosophy, or even nonphilosophical thought. The essential possibilities of thinking have been too thoroughly exhausted —as Heidegger points out—and the paths of thought too well trodden—as Heidegger often ignores—for him to be able to do that.

To put Heidegger's overcoming of metaphysics into its proper—paradoxical—perspective, one has to balance his not too well founded charge against the history of philosophy with another one that he conspicuously fails to make. He charges that metaphysics, or humanistic philosophy, is so preoccupied with beings—human or other—and *their* Being that it fails to think of Being as such. But he consistently avoids mention of the opposite danger for philosophy: the exclusive preoccupation with Being as such that fails to think of beings—human or other—and of Being as the Being of *beings*. And this oversight proves to be fatal for the last stage of his "philosophy." For philosophy has not just one but two limits, and one cannot transcend either without transcending not just a branch or type of philosophy —humanistic metaphysics—but all responsible philosophical thought.

Heidegger is quite right in saying that the essential possibilities of metaphysics have been exhausted. Not only metaphysics, but philosophy as such has always moved between the two poles or limits just mentioned: on the one hand the preoccupation with the beings we encounter, and the beings we are, in everyday experience, a preoccupation that is all too aware of diversity and multiplicity but fails to think of the common ground that underlies all diversity, the unity that overarches all multiplicity; on the other hand the obsessive preoccupation with ultimate Unity that fails to think of the multiplicity and diversity of the beings with whose Being we are concerned. One can easily classify traditional philosophers by noting which of these two poles, the Many or the One, the concrete or the abstract, the particular or the universal, the empirical or the ideal, the immanent or the Transcendent, they were most concerned with. But it is even more important to note that all philosophers worthy of the name have been concerned with both; that these two poles between which philosophy moves—and of which Heidegger mentions only one—represent the limits of philosophy, i.e. that all the essential possibilities of philosophy lie between them, and that they therefore cannot be transcended *within philosophy*. The closer one approaches either one of them and fails to think of the other, the more one relinquishes philosophy in favor of something else: an all too empirical, possibly technological, allegedly practical thinking (the danger Heidegger emphasizes), or an all too empty and formal, though often emotionally charged and mystical-religious, thinking of absolute unity (the danger Heidegger is oblivious of and consequently succumbs to).

Heidegger has indeed succeeded in showing these limits and demonstrating these dangers, but he did so in a philosophical-unphilosophical manner: partly by his constant (philosophical) awareness of the one, but partly by his (unphilosophical) overstepping of the other; partly by his following in the footsteps of traditional philosophers, but partly by his returning to the nonphilosophical sources and offshoots of philosophical thought. We can learn from both of these steps, but we cannot at the same time accept Heidegger's claim that, overstepping the limits of responsible thought in his latest writings, he is opening up new paths for philosophy. What he is doing now is neither new nor philosophy.

So, as regards Heidegger's overcoming of humanistic metaphysics, there is this to say: in the first two stages of his thought—from *Being and Time* to *Thought*—he fails to accomplish his aim and remains, by and large, within the philosophical (metaphysical, humanistic) tradition. In the last stage he succeeds, but in doing so he fails as a philosopher. For there is no such thing as an "overcoming of metaphysics" in philosophy.

This is not hard to see when one reflects on what exactly

metaphysics, humanism, and subjectivism mean for Heidegger.

Metaphysics is an interpretation of Being on the basis of beings, a preoccupation with the Being of *beings* that is oblivious of Being as such. Subjectivistic humanism is an interpretation of Being on the basis of man's understanding of Being, a preoccupation with man that makes man, the human subject, the ultimate subject: the measure and ground of all disclosure. Now how could thought ever overcome this type of thinking and still remain thought?

As Heidegger himself once pointed out, we have no immediate approach to Being and no immediate vision of the Absolute. "The Overt itself is the Immediate. No mediate being, be it a god or a man, can therefore ever attain the Immediate immediately" (*E* 59); "the Immediate . . . incloses in itself all·fullness and structure, and is thus unapproachable by isolated beings, be they gods or men. The Holy, as the Unapproachable, throws every immediate intrusion of the mediate [men and gods] out of its intended course [and casts it] into futility. The Holy places all experience outside its habituation and thus deprives it of a place where it could stand. Thus dis-possessing (*entsetzend*) the Holy is Terror (*das Entsetzliche*) itself." In other words, an immediate vision of the Absolute is not only unattainable but also undesirable for finite—mediate—beings. It is a terrible possession that could only dispossess, unhinge, dis-tract us, for, approaching Being, man only faces the Abyss: no longer confronted with beings, he is confronted not with Being itself but with a void that the intellect cannot endure. Being as such, should men ever try to approach it immediately, is sheer terror to the intellect, a terror that threatens our humanity (finite vision); it is the Infinite that offers reason no grasp or hold and leaves it foundering and groundless.

But if an immediate vision of Being is unattainable, we can approach Being only mediately, metaphysically, through beings. If a nonhuman, more than human vision of Being is unattainable, we can reveal Being only mediately —humanistically, subjectively—i.e. through the medium and mediation of the human understanding. Being is never given, to us, in itself. It is given through beings alone, and this mediate givenness is not only the way in which Being is *first* given, revealed, disclosed, a way we can somehow transcend, by way of mediation, in the course of a long dialectic ascent or descent. Being is given, disclosed, first and last, only in and through beings, and no effort of human thought can transcend this manner of Being and go beyond the Being of beings to Being as such.

Human thought—as Heidegger shows in *Being and Time* —is a *Be-dingen,* a projecting of conditions of possibility, of limiting horizons of Being. Thus absolutely uncondi- tioned, unlimited, horizon- and form-less Being can never be thought. Thought is a *dialegesthai,* a making of distinctions, a marking of limits, a separating and com- bining, a comparison, and thus the utterly undifferentiated, indefinite, and undistinguishable (Being as such) cannot be thought. Thought is analysis and synthesis, an unfolding of structures in their organic unity and differentiation; it is literally ex-plication and articulation. Therefore it cannot think of Being as such: the unmetaphysical, unarticulated, unexplicated, and inexplicable One. Being as transcendent par excellence—for this is what unmetaphysical Being means—is unthinkable; it is thinkable only in reference to what it transcends (beings). Being as absolute—as ab-solved from all beings—is an empty negative concept, and all attempts to think it positively are self-contradictory. (As Plato well knew. But Heidegger no longer quotes the *Sophist* when he attempts to talk of Being as an Unfolding apart from what it unfolds into, as a Ground apart from what is grounded in it, as One apart from the Many, as Identity or Difference as such apart from the identical and the different.)

Since we have no access to Being other than human thought, no disclosure other than human disclosure, philosophy necessarily remains humanistic and meta-physical: a movement within the hermeneutic circle—an unfolding of *man's* understanding of Being as the Being of *beings* into which it unfolds—and not a going beyond.

Heidegger is very fond of using metaphorical expressions like *Ereignis* (from *er-aeugen*), shining (*scheinen: Schoene*), appearing, light, and enlightenment, in reference to truth and Being. But it is characteristic of his last writings that in them he seems to forget where these metaphors have been taken from and what they imply. Metaphors have meaning and impact only by virtue of their origin, and it is a sign of Heidegger's growing insensitivity even to language that he tends to be more and more oblivious of the etymological origin of his key terms, and lets himself be seduced by his metaphors far beyond the realm where they could still carry him. He objects to Plato's metaphoric *idea* that it makes Being too relative to our *idein* or sight, but he ignores the fact that almost the entire complex of his terms comes from the same metaphoric region which is precisely the metaphysical, humanistic region he tries to transcend. "Vision," "view," "disclosure," and "revela-tion" are, after all, only possible if something is visible, at view, disclosed, and revealed; and something can be disclosed or revealed only *as* something, i.e. within defining limits, boundaries, and horizons that make it appear as this definite, limited, finite thing rather than nothing at all. In other words, even in terms of Heidegger's metaphors disclosure must be meta-physical: a disclosure in and through beings (*meta ta physika onta*). Pure light as such is invisible; light has to be reflected in and by something to be seen. Pure enlightenment—that is not enlightenment of and about something—is unenlightening; pure revelation —that is not the revelation of something—is no revelation; and pure disclosure—without anything being disclosed—is no disclosure at all. In terms of Heidegger's metaphors, Being can shine forth and be seen only through beings— the limited, particular, differentiated many—and never in itself. Visibility implies horizons, finitude, and limitation, and what is utterly limitless and formless—as the Being that is not the Being of beings must be—is not open to sight. There can be no truth—*aletheia*—without the appearance and disclosedness of beings, and, since for Heidegger Being is truth, there can be no Being without beings.

The same metaphors make all revelation humanistic and subjectivistic. For sight, disclosure, vision, etc. necessarily imply—as much as Plato's *idea* does—a seer, a being to whom something can appear and be revealed. But then, Being can no more be (revealed) without men than it can be without beings, and one cannot overcome the humanism, subjectivism, and relativism of *Being and Time*.

It is not without trepidation that one accuses Heidegger, the erstwhile master and perhaps most creative contemporary user of the German language, of "insensitivity to language." Nevertheless his mounting violence toward language cannot be ignored, especially as his "metaphoric" difficulties are an illustration of, indeed but another aspect of, his metaphysical difficulties. Heidegger's "going beyond metaphysics" would require a corresponding going beyond language, a complete relinquishing of the use of words that have meaning within, and only within, the disclosure of a world and in reference to the beings in the world thus disclosed. But such a language—that might truly be the abode of Being rather than of man only—is not only not available; its very concept is self-contradictory, is at best a mere limiting concept, a negative concept to language as world-disclosure. After his conversion Heidegger complained that the language of *Being and Time* was the language of metaphysics and was thus inadequate to what he really wanted to say. But his real trouble is that any language qua language is metaphysical—a finite disclosure of Being within finite horizons of disclosure—and Heidegger's attempts to ignore this only result in straining language beyond its limits and producing a welter of ambiguity, obscurity, contradiction, and paradox rather than meaningful disclosure. Even the fact that this procedure does not result in utter meaninglessness is merely the consequence of Heidegger's failure rather than success in achieving his aim: while he insists that he wants nothing more than to uproot his metaphors from the soil that hitherto nourished them and to divorce *his* meaning from *worldly* meaning, he is, as might have been expected, not altogether successful in this, and his words still retain a residue of the meaning he seeks to cancel.

To appreciate the futility of Heidegger's attempt at overcoming metaphysics, we have to distinguish between philosophical and nonphilosophical transcendence. Philosophically one can transcend beings as well as the close confines of one's own uninstructed vision, i.e. one can transcend the limited horizons of any particular disclosure of any particular individual human being. Metaphysics is nothing but the process of this transcendence, and it has been such long before Kant's "transcendental" philosophy. But philosophical transcendence means a transcendence *of* (any and all particular) beings *to* their common underlying ground, a transcendence *of* a too narrow (individual and particular) subjectivity *to* intersubjectivity: our shared horizons of experience. Such a transcendence, of all objects of experience and of all particular experiencing subjects, by way of a reflection on experience as finite horizon-

projecting and image-making, is designed to reveal not
Being or Truth as such but our finite ways and modes of
disclosing beings. As such, this kind of transcendence
reflects us back into rather than carries us beyond the realm
of beings it clarifies, and it reflects us back into common
human experience rather than carries us beyond it. It is in
this (transcendental) return to what is transcended (objects
and subjects) that the meaning and utility of metaphysical
transcendence lies.

But a nonmetaphysical transcendence not only of beings
but also of the Being of beings to Being as such, not only of
individual and therefore possibly nonshareable modes of
disclosure, but of all human disclosure to Disclosure (pure,
unconditioned, unlimited) as such, the transcendence
Heidegger aims at and, in the end, almost accomplishes,
involves the transcendence of all meaning whatsoever.
Such transcendence, as Heidegger's latest writings show,
does not enable the entrance into a new realm of disclosure;
it merely transports us beyond all disclosure and revelation.

Attempts at a nonmetaphysical transcendence are a great
danger for philosophy because they are a built-in danger:
they are but a radicalization, an extreme form, of metaphysical transcendence; the transcendence of (particular)
beings to (their) Being is stretched here to its breaking point
in the concept of (an absolutely transcendent) Being as
such. But precisely because the danger is great we have to
recognize it and guard against it.

All great philosophers knew the restlessness of human
reason, its urge to go to the limits of its own finitude and,
in the end, to transcend them. But while these men felt the
power of this urge they resisted its compulsion and saw the
futility and philosophically self-defeating nature of a leap
beyond the edge of rationality. They all knew that philosophical dialectic can carry one only to the limits of thought
and not beyond. Even Hegel, whose attempt "to leap over

one's own shadow" (*FD* 161)—as Heidegger lucidly characterizes it—came closest to success, did not try to cut off the Absolute from its conditioned and limited manifestations—as Heidegger now attempts to do—but, instead of going beyond the limits of thought, merely imposed these limits on what supposedly lay beyond them. Heidegger knows this, and, speaking of Hegel, recognizes the urge, the attempt, and the failure: "Hegel alone has seemingly succeeded in leaping over this shadow—but only by eliminating this shadow, i.e. the finitude of man, and leaping into the sun itself. Hegel has leaped over the shadow but he has not thereby cleared the shadow. Nonetheless every philosopher *must* want to do this. This must is his call" (*FD* 161, Heidegger's italics). But it is one thing to recognize this all too human urge, and quite another to abandon oneself to it so completely that one is, like Heidegger, carried away far beyond the realm of responsible thought.

Heidegger is right in calling thought's demand for transcendence a "must" for philosophers. Philosophy is kept alive by the demand of thought to transcend not only beings but also its hitherto accepted limits, rules, and categories. Only by going to the limits of thought can philosophy ever know these limits as well as the region they limit: the area of human knowledge, the legitimate region of use of the categories of thought. And only by going to these limits again and again can human thought appropriate, possibly modify, but at any rate keep alive its own rules and forms. But Heidegger fails in not recognizing this demand as the temptation it can so easily become when it is not curbed: the temptation of thought to go beyond any and all limits of thought so as to think something that cannot be thought. Unmindful of Plato's warning against gazing too directly into the sun, he succumbs to the temptation, and the result is not a heightened, nonhuman clarity of sight but rather an all too predictable blindness to what might have been visible. Unmindful of Kant's warning against extending the categories of thought beyond their legitimate use, he succumbs to the temptation, and the result is not a further, postcategorical, nonmetaphysical insight, but a mere transcendental illusion on his part.

Instead of thinking metaphysically and humanistically, and thereby making thought responsible to itself, Heidegger tries to think nonmetaphysically and nonhumanistically, in order to make human thought responsible—a response—to something Wholly Other. But in this he fails, for he fails to adopt the only appropriate response to what is Wholly Other: utter silence.

Beyond Good and Evil

The problems of truth and Being are inseparable from the problem of the truth of existence, and thus all ontology has ethical implications. What then are the results of Heidegger's overcoming of humanistic metaphysics as regards his theory of man?

In the preceding I have tried to show that in the first and, to an extent, the second stage of his hermeneutic Heidegger fails to overcome metaphysics, while in the last he almost succeeds but in the process fails as a philosopher. His overcoming of a humanistic ethics functions similarly. The first—and possibly the second—stage of his hermeneutic is humanistic, though not sufficiently so to be ethically adequate, while the last stage is nonhumanistic, and in consequence fails to provide a basis for an acceptable theory of man.

Heidegger's existentialistic analysis—*Being and Time*—is, in a sense, a thoroughly humanistic theory. As an investigation of the structure of human existence it is but a manifestation and radicalization of humanism: man's preoccupation with his own Being. As a characterization of Dasein qua an existential, purposive, aim-directed being, whose concern about its own Being guides and permeates all its disclosure, it makes humanism—precisely this concern—equivalent to humanity, the essence of man. Caught in the "hermeneutic circle," *Being and Time* in effect revolves in a humanistic circle.

So far, the humanism of *Being and Time* is unobjectionable. For what could be of more concern to man than to clarify his own existence, what could be more sensible than to try to define human existence on the basis of an investigation precisely of human existence, and what could be more reasonable than a definition of the humanity of man precisely as humanism, this preoccupation with our nature that the investigation investigates and manifests at the same time?

The trouble with Heidegger's existentialistic analysis is not that it is humanistic, but that it is not humanistic enough: for all its preoccupation with man it does not go far enough in clarifying, and providing guidance for, human existence.

In *Being and Time* Heidegger distinguishes between "authentic" and "unauthentic" existence. Dasein exists authentically when it discloses to itself its own possibilities of Being on its own and as its own, and projects itself into its self-disclosed possibilities. Authentic existence is the "truth" of existence: Dasein is disclosed (true) to itself as well as true to its own self-disclosed Being. Unauthentic existence is the opposite of this. Submerged in the "publicity of the one," unauthentic Dasein accepts uncritically the commonly accepted interpretations of what it means to be a human being, and thus fails to appropriate—disclose and really make its own—its own existence; undisclosed to itself Dasein is untrue to its own possibilities and inadequate to its own life.

This distinction between authentic and unauthentic existence, though not altogether novel, is a useful one. But does Heidegger provide any practical guidance for becoming authentic?

Authentic existence in *Being and Time* is the result of "authentic resolve": Dasein's coming face to face with death as its own inalienable and inevitable extreme possibility. Facing death as its own, Dasein supposedly understands life as its own: as its own inalienable possibility which no one can realize for it and which it therefore has to realize itself. Facing death as its extreme possibility, i.e. as the end of all its possibilities, Dasein becomes conscious of the urgency of realizing these possibilities, and is thereby moved to projecting itself into them. This is the way Dasein supposedly becomes authentic in resolute existence. But does authentic resolve really work?

In *Being and Time* Heidegger fails to show how unauthentic man, from whose thinking nothing is further removed than any thought of his own inexorably approaching death, who flees nothing with more violence and greater fear than the threat of his own extinction, who suppresses nothing with more urgency than the intimation of his own inevitable end, will suddenly bring up the resolution to be resolute. Man is unauthentic precisely because he lacks this resolution, because the public "one does not allow the courage to dread death emerge" (*BT* 254/298). If so, what will make him suddenly resolute? If man is truly "fallen" (*verfallen*), what will enable him to perform the extremely difficult feat of being-unto-death, against which his whole unauthentic existence is a protest? Will resolution come to him as a thief in the night to steal away his fears of fearing death? Will the voice of Being suddenly call upon him and call him to reckoning, break down his defenses and expose him naked to his own existence? So it seems in *Being and Time*. The "call of conscience" comes upon man "against all expectation and against our will" (*BT* 275/320), it is a call that is "never planned, prepared, or willingly accomplished by ourselves" (ibid.), a call that supposedly comes from the depth of our Being but still "falls upon us" (ibid.) without our doing, from above and beyond us, as it were.

This being so, *Being and Time* already foreshadows some aspects of Heidegger's latest development. For if such calls that come to man in the small hours of the night come without his having called them forth, if these voices that he has not invoked summon him as if from outside—for they are beyond *his* power—then already in *Being and Time* man can do little more than wait for the call of Being. Indeed, since there is nothing he could do to make himself resolute, and since this resolution will resolve, if and when it comes, everything without his active participation, he might as well forget about waiting and live his life without any ultimate care and concern—as indeed he does in unauthentic existence. He is helpless on his own, and what will help him does not need his help. Even if the resolution resulting from such call should truly be a resolution to *his own* existence, it could hardly be called *man's authentic* (his own) resolve. It comes from beyond man—since it is beyond his power—and Heidegger's reliance on some such power beyond man's own makes *Being and Time* incapable of being the basis of any theory of true ethical education. The work provides no method whereby man can be helped —let alone help himself—to grow to the full stature of authentic existence.

But this is not the worst of Heidegger's shortcomings. For if his latest prophecies are truly inspired—and one could hardly *prove* that they are not—such calls might come. But even if they did, and resolution came to man by the grace of Being, would such resolution really resolve anything and make Dasein authentic? What would happen in unauthentic Dasein's sudden confrontation with its own death?

Surely the appalling thought of death as the irresistibly

approaching and inevitable end of life would quicken one's sense of life; it would lend existence an extraordinary sense of urgency, a consciousness of now or never. But would it do more than that, would it actually help us make any concrete resolutions, and would such resolutions once made be necessarily authentic? This is to be doubted.

To begin with, the urgency the thought of death lends life is quite general and indefinite; it makes life as such urgent but fails to disclose what in particular is truly urgent in my life. Heidegger himself insists that the call of conscience that calls man into facing death as his own tells him nothing, gives him no information; " 'nothing' is called to the self that is called" (*BT* 273/318), the "call speaks in the eerie mode of silence" (*BT* 277/322), it simply calls the self "to its own self" (*BT* 273/318). Therefore, facing death may make me aware of the fact that my life has to be lived and lived by me, but not of what exactly the particular life that is to be lived by me is. It may bring home the fact of my finitude in general (that I will not live forever and therefore have to live now), but not what I as a particular finite being am. It may make me aware of my ultimate limit (death) but not of my particular ones, of my temporal end but not of my particular ends, of my purposiveness in general but not of my particular purposes. As such, being-unto-death is an ultimate definition of (a setting limits to) my existence that, in effect, fails to define it, as to content, in any way whatsoever.

Heidegger rightly sees that facing death in all its threatening imminence will make our immediate cares and concerns irrelevant, break down our unthinking routine, lift us out of our often unessential relations to the beings (human or other) in our world, and thus it may well be the first step toward resolutions that will make our existence more authentic. But what Heidegger fails to see is that this is all that facing death can be and do. It can momentarily free us from (possibly unessential) involvements and thus free us for (possibly more essential) new involvements, but it cannot free us, i.e. deliver us, into our essential involvements (the ones we should be actually involved in because we are already—by nature—thrown into, involved in, them), because it fails to disclose them, and thus fails to disclose ourselves to ourselves.

Heidegger's "authenticity" of existence is, after all, but a new name for the age-old concept of *arete:* the excellence in being what one is, the fulfillment of one's own particular functions; true self-realization in the sense of self-disclosure and self-fulfillment. Authenticity is a demand for man because human Dasein is characterized by both facticity and existentiality: it has necessary possibilities (functions to fulfill), but these possibilities that it is "thrown into" are not already realized (by nature) but have to be realized—disclosed and fulfilled—by Dasein itself, and Dasein is aware of this fact.

But being-unto-death will not help us become authentic because it will not give us any insight into our essential functions. Urging us to decision but not to any particular decision, making it clear that we must choose but not what —let alone how—we must choose, being merely "a choice of this choice, the decision for being able to be oneself on one's own" (*BT* 268/313) but not a revelation of what this self is, facing death will bring us to the brink of resolution but it will leave us there hovering, completely irresolute. It will detach us from the (possibly unauthentic) life we lead, detach us from other human beings, detach us from the things of this world, but precisely because it will do so it will not rightly detach us from our detachment and lead us back into a more authentic life.

In effect, being-unto-death volatilizes our existence rather than makes it concrete, and the uniqueness (*Jemeinigkeit*) it supposedly provides is no more than an empty concept, the emotional version of a Kantian transcendental idea. To be a unique self, I need to realize not only that no one can die my death and thus no one can live my life for me, but also what exactly I as a supposedly unique individual self am. To be a finite self I have to realize not only that I have to die and thus must live while I can, but also what exactly my finite limits and potentialities of life are. Authenticity does not come from a merely negative realization (of the necessity and imminence of death) and a merely negative movement (away from my present projects, concerns, involvements). It requires a positive realization (of what I truly am) and a positive movement (back into a more essential life). And Heidegger's "authentic resolve" in the face of death does not provide these. Therefore in practice it will not only fail to make me unique: it will fail to make me even a particular human being because it abstracts (me) from all my particular concerns[4] and thus in fact it abstracts "me" (a supposedly unique and inalienable but in fact completely empty self) from myself. I am a self not so much in my relation to my own death as in the totality of my temporal cares and concerns, in the whole of my worldly relations to other beings in my world. It is only in and through these that I can be related to myself—to a self that is more than an empty idea—and being-unto-death, isolating "me" from all my worldly relations, hides rather than reveals these— and thus myself—to me.

To be sure, the confrontation with death will not leave us permanently suspended in a state of indecision and inaction. Its very urgency will soon plunge us back into life. But, since facing death does not of itself give our resolution any content, this urgency is blind and direction- less, and thus our reentry into worldly existence will be more of a headlong flight into the first best possibility of

4. For Heidegger, it is only in unauthentic existence that " 'one is' what one does" (BT 239/283).

Being, into any possibility at all, than a choice of one's true self; it will be more an escape from irresoluteness than an authentic resolution. Heidegger's authentic resolve in the face of death is, therefore, not just empty—making us free for, open to, decision, but leaving the decision itself completely open—it is also dangerous. It leads to a blind leap and—if resoluteness implies steadfastness in what is resolved—a blind adherence. It is more of a hindrance than a help to authentic existence.

What Heidegger's insistence on resolute decisions, on the choosing of choice, leaves completely out of account is that authenticity is not necessarily achieved by *my* choosing a way of life for myself—rather than following the "one"—and abiding by my choice; it is achieved, rather, by my adoption of the way of life that is—already, potentially—my own and therefore necessary for me to adopt. Were not some particular finite possibilities of Being more essential for me than others (since I am already factually projected in them although I have not yet realized them existentially) the choice would be meaningless, since no choice, even the "choice not to choose," could possibly be wrong, and authentic existence would be neither a problem nor an existential demand for man. But if choices are meaningful and authenticity is a problem for man, then being-unto-death is no solution to the problem even though it results in resolutions. For what makes resolutions authentic is not that *I* happened to make them but that they were the right ones for me to make. And it is not the urgency of the decision—in the face of death—that makes my decision right—essential for me—but the much more difficult process of cool deliberation: reflection on life as a rich and varied complex of possibilities rather than just on death as their ultimate end and negation. Such reflection requires not so much the facing of an indefinite future as it requires the facing of a definite past: an examination of the many particular concrete possibilities into which I have already projected myself but which have left me unfulfilled and unwhole, thereby indicating, on examination, my need for further self-projection. Being-unto-death does not in itself promote such rational self-examination; it only makes death loom larger and larger till death "reveals itself as something that knows no measure" (*BT* 262/307) and our dread becomes correspondingly boundless. Such dreadful measurelessness is hardly the climate for the sober measuring that leads to authentic resolutions.

Heidegger's failure to provide a practical process and usable criteria for distinguishing between authentic and unauthentic possibilities of Being turns even the virtues of *Being and Time* into vices. For without offering a way to authentic existence it is pointless to oppose "publicity" and to insist on *Jemeinigkeit*. Such opposition and insistence merely hide the fact that I am not only different but also in many respects like my fellow men (whose "public" norms and ways of life can therefore never be totally wrong for me), and that I can be authentic not because any concrete possibilities I may possibly project myself into are irreduplicable—none in fact is—but because certain possibilities of Being happen to be *my own* and are therefore necessary for me to realize. I can realize (disclose and fulfill) them, however, only in an active dialogue and dialectic relationship with others as well as with myself, and being-unto-death puts an end to all such dialectic.[5] It isolates the "self" so completely that in this isolation the self is almost completely destroyed; it is a "self-encounter" in which the self encounters literally nothing. What saves the self from utter destruction and annihilation in the face

5. "In its encounter with itself all of its [Dasein's] relations to other Dasein are dissolved" (*BT* 250/294), "Dasein is isolated upon itself" (*BT* 263/308) but no "dialogue with itself" is initiated within the self (*BT* 273/318).

of death is that "publicity," the unquestioning acceptance
of communal norms and values, is replaced in *Being and
Time* by an equally uncritical, and even more haphazard,
fortuitous, and harmful resolve. But this is hardly an advance on what Heidegger opposes.

For all of Heidegger's conversion of thought from Dasein
to Being, the ethical implications of his latest writings closely
resemble those of *Being and Time;* the only difference is that
what was implicit in *Being and Time* becomes quite explicit
and unmistakable in *Toward Language, Gelassenheit,* and
Nothing Is without Ground.

In *Being and Time,* Dasein was lifted out of its everyday
existence and brought face to face with death by a mysterious "call of conscience" rather than by its own effort. Just
such a call of an equally mysterious Being, rather than man's
own doing, accomplishes the same result in the latest
writings. In *Being and Time* the call of conscience called
nothing whatsoever to Dasein but simply called to it in
silence. Just such a silent call is the Voice of Being now.
Being-unto-death was a completely empty self-encounter
in which Dasein in fact encountered nothing. No more is
encountered in man's facing his ultimate Ground; he still
faces a void. In being-unto-death, death revealed itself as
something that knew no measure. The abysmal Ground to
which we abandon ourselves in *Gelassenheit* is equally
measureless and unbounded.

Since facing death gave our resolutions no content,
resolve (*Entschlossenheit*) was a mere choice of choice, an
open decision that could be given any content. The same
openness characterizes our "openness to the Mystery," our
"dis-closure" (*Ent-schlossenheit*) to the "Overt Itself." It is
a waiting—we do not know for what—that in effect discloses
nothing and thus can be filled—if it is to be filled at all—
with any content whatsoever. Neither resolve, nor this new

dis-closure leads to rational decision, ethical rules, and law. The urgency of our relationship to our ultimate end (death) was liable to force us into an unguided leap into any possibility of existence whatever, and thus our resolve resulted in a blind decision and a blind adherence. Our relationship to our ultimate Ground begins and ends as an unguided leap into the Abyss, a blind trust in and devotion to something unknown and unseen. Both attitudes are characterized by a kind of Kierkegaardian despair of infinitude due to lack of finitude, a despair of possibility due to lack of necessity.

Heidegger insists on the unauthenticity or unessentiality of our everyday existence in both *Being and Time* and his latest writings, but in neither does he offer anything but a vague hope and a directionless doctrine of salvation. He keeps exhorting man to change his life, but nowhere shows a way toward this transformation. He speaks of correspondence between Being and man, and fondly quotes Hoelderlin's dictum "we are a dialogue," but a true dialogue—with himself or with Being—that could make man correspond —to himself or to Being as such—is absent from both extremes of his work.

What mainly distinguishes Heidegger's solution to the problem of man in *Being and Time* from that in his latest writings is that the latter is even more of a negative solution and, if possible, even less a solution than the former. For while in *Being and Time* Heidegger's panacea to human existence—being-unto-death—brought man to a negative realization (of the necessary and imminent end of our existence) and a negative movement (away from our present concerns), and thus failed to reflect man back into an authentic existence, its aim, at least, was nothing but this: to make man authentic here and now, as a worldly being, in the totality of his temporal relationships and concerns. But the latest writings no longer even have this aim; they not only fail to make man an authentic Being-in-the-world, they are altogether opposed to authenticity. They not only negate our present concerns, they negate human life—as a worldly concern for one's Being—altogether. Instead of reminding us of the eventual end of our existence and exhorting us to make something out of our lives here and now, they insist on the nullity of all merely human existence. These writings do not merely fail in giving directions for life; they are opposed to all such direction and direct man, instead, away from this life, and toward a wholly other, ineffable kind of Being.

Being and Time was humanistic in intention—in that it was a preoccupation with man that attempted to clarify his Being on the basis of a reflection on worldly existence—but not humanistic enough in its results—in that it failed to show the way to a truly human existence. The latest writings, explicitly attempting to reverse the trend of *Being and Time,* are inversely characterized: they are nonhumanistic in intention—ostensibly preoccupied with a nonhuman, wholly other Being, they aim to clarify man's existence on the basis of what is wholly other—though not altogether in their result—in that they fail to achieve it. In consequence *Being and Time* offered man a way of salvation that did not lead to its humanistic aim—authentic human existence—and thus was not worth following. The last writings attempt to offer a way of salvation that has no humanistic aim and is therefore impossible for man to follow.

In a way, Heidegger's progress from *Being and Time* to *Gelassenheit* and *Nothing Is without Ground* has its own logic. In *Being and Time* Heidegger placed man in the absolute center of his own (man's) thought in order to clarify human existence from within, anthropocentrically, as it were, by circling around man himself. Since this attempt failed, he took the opposite course: he placed something wholly other than human in the center, and hoped to illumine human existence ecstatically, by stepping out of it altogether and throwing a more than human light upon it from without. There is nothing wrong with the logic of this movement of reversal; what is wrong is simply one of its premises. But this makes Heidegger's whole conversion a kind of error and erring: a movement that moves from a false premise, through twisted paths, to a paradoxical conclusion.

The basic premise of Heidegger's conversion or reversal is that (since *Being and Time* failed and *Being and Time* was humanistic) with the failure of *Being and Time* humanism as such failed. But this is an unacceptable premise. *Being and Time* failed to provide solutions to the problem of human existence not because it was humanistic but because it was not humanistic enough, i.e. because, in spite of its humanistic beginning, in one respect—in its proposal of a way to authentic existence—it already antici-pated the nonhumanistic standpoint of the latest writings.

Being and Time correctly defined man as the being concerned about its own Being, the being whose essence is self-directed questioning, a progressive self-disclosure of and self-projection into its self-disclosed possibilities of Being. But when it came to finding a way in which to make man essential, Heidegger almost completely ignored his own definition of the essence of man—as involved in a self-directed questioning—and proposed a way that was in effect the opposite of all existential, self-reflective, self-disclosing dialogue: being-unto-death, the facing of the negation of all of Dasein's possibilities, which lifted man out of his questioning of and preoccupation with his worldly possi-bilities, disclosed nothing about the self, and put an end to, rather than promoted, rational self-reflection. In *Being and Time* Heidegger had characterized man as an onto-logical being—one whose essence is to understand its Being—but in spite of this he proposed a solution to man's problems—measureless dread in the face of an equally measureless threat—that precluded all understanding. He described man as a teleological, aim-directed, purposive being, but he forgot that one important component of being teleological is *logos,* a rational comprehension of one's aim and purpose and a rational search for and calculation of ways and means to attain it. This omission of, and indeed outright opposition to, rationality on Heidegger's part in effect anticipated his attitude toward reason and understanding in the latest writings, and it was this anticipation of the conclusions of his last hermeneutic period in the first that accounted for the ethical failure of *Being and Time.* But this anticipation—that the essence of man was not existentiality, ontology, and teleology, but the life without why, and that therefore the way to become essential was an unquestioning leap and a blind trust in something beyond man—was not humanistic; it was directly contradictory to the humanistic definition of man. Thus Heidegger's conclusion, that a conversion from humanism to nonhumanism was necessary, was the necessary result of the presupposition of the (nonhumanistic) conclusion in the argument for it.

The circularity of Heidegger's conversion—of his own failure to elaborate a truly humanistic philosophy into the failure of humanism as such—is highly deplorable for two reasons: it led to an impossible demand (for nonhumanistic definitions of man and Being, and for a nonhuman existence), and it led away from a real demand (for self-fulfillment here and now) and a usable definition of man on whose basis an ethics designed for human use could have been developed.

In his last writings Heidegger is intent on getting away from an immanent definition of man, and on defining man's essence on the basis of an independent definition of Being. But this attempt to overcome humanism proves to be as futile as the one at overcoming metaphysics. In the first place, as I have tried to show in the preceding section, we have no direct access to the Absolute and cannot therefore attain to a nonmetaphysical, nonhumanistic definition of Being. This absence of an independent (of man) definition of Being makes a nonhumanistic definition of man (based on an independent, nonhumanistic definition of Being) equally unattainable, and turns our efforts at obtaining one into the paradoxical effort to define something unknown but knowable (man or Being as disclosed by the human understanding) on the basis of something not only unknown but also utterly unknowable and undefinable (absolutely transcendent Being as such).

In the second place, even if we had a supposedly independent definition of Being—by way of a direct revelation such as all religions lay a claim to and, in the end, Heidegger arrogates—this would not get us any closer to a nonhumanistic definition of man, or even of Being. For any definition of Being would have to be comprehensible to man—in order to *define* Being for man—and would thus have to be given in human rather than nonhuman terms. Being may well be Wholly Other in itself; but if we are to hearken to it and respond to its Voice it must not speak *to us* in a wholly other tongue.[6] And even if it did, its Message would still have to be translated into human language and intepreted by a human interpreter before it could be a message to us. Consequently any definition of the essence of man, based on such a definition of Being, would already be an immanent, man-bound, humanistic definition—based on *man's* understanding of Being—rather than a transcendent, nonhumanistic one—over and above and beyond man's understanding.

6. Cf. K. Loewith, *Geschichtliche Abhandlungen* (Stuttgart, Kohlhammer, 1960), p. 212. My indebtedness to Loewith in this chapter is greater than can be indicated by individual footnotes.

Heidegger's search for a nonhumanistic definition of man and Being merely manifests and reinforces what it attempts to deny and refute. The search for a new (be it ever so nonhumanistic) definition of Being is, after all, but a manifestation of the existentiality and ontological nature of man (his search for his own Being) that the search is supposed to overcome. Thus it is a self-refuting search, for, seeking for such a definition, Heidegger is engaged in an enterprise which, in accordance with the definition sought, is totally unessential for man, whose essence is now defined as the life without questioning and defining. Whatever content the new definition has is derived from its negative reference to what it tries to transcend (human existence humanistically comprehended) rather than from any insight into what it tries to attain (nonhumanistic Being as such). The whole enterprise escapes total meaninglessness only by virtue of its indirect description as well as manifestation of our humanistic, ontological, metaphysical nature, against which it is directed. Thus, while *Being and Time* failed because and to the extent that it anticipated the nonhumanistic turn of the latest writings, these writings do not fail altogether (to have some meaning) because and to the extent that they manifest and indirectly reinforce (against Heidegger's explicit intention) the humanistic spirit of the earlier ones, from which they still draw inspiration and meaning.

This extent is, of course, not considerable. It is just enough to make Heidegger's latest writings paradoxical rather than completely meaningless. His proposal for a more essential (nonhumanistic) human existence is not meaningless, for its meaning is supplied by its negation of human existence as we know it here and now. But it is therefore paradoxical, because it counsels the overcoming of our very humanity as the way to true humanity.

In *Being and Time* Heidegger saw clearly that it is our

ontological, teleological, existential nature (concern for and
questioning of our Being) that makes existence problematic,
i.e. makes man a problem for himself. In his later writings
he showed that no ultimate solution to this problem can be
provided by the thing that creates the problem in the first
place, i.e. that our ontological nature (questioning of our
own Being) precludes rather than provides a final solution
that would put an end to this questioning. On the one hand,
the reasons reason gives (*reddit*) to reason (the demand for
reasons) are always adequate to reason, for they are given
in its own terms and thus cannot help answering its particular demands. On the other hand, they can never be totally
adequate to reason and answer its ultimate demand (for
ultimate reasons), because they are grounded in reason and
thus cannot serve as a "grounding ground" for it. Therefore rational human existence (our ontological nature)
cannot of itself overcome its ultimate groundlessness and
find, on its own and by its own effort, an unshakeable
foundation on which to rest.

Faced with this ultimate groundlessness and restlessness
of reason, in his latest writings Heidegger provides the only
logical solution to the problem (a solution that was, however, implicit in *Being and Time's* resolve in the face of
death): if reason makes existence a problem which it cannot
ultimately solve, the only solution to the problem is to
abandon reason. If our existentiality or ontological nature
leads to existential and ontological predicaments which it
cannot help man to overcome completely, the solution is
to overcome and relinquish our existential-ontological
nature. If our being-in-the-truth (disclosure of Being-in-
the-world) is always and inevitably a being-in-the-untruth
(limited revelation within finite horizons of disclosure), the
way out of this "untrue" state of Being is to abandon this
type of truth or disclosure—questioning of Being—and
abandon ourselves to the life without why. Oedipus' sight,

his self-disclosing passion, apparently brought him to grief. So let us put out our eyes and go to Colonus, where the grace of Being is waiting.

This solution is, of course, perfect and unexceptionable as a solution to the problem. The only trouble is that it does not happen to be a *human* solution, a solution to *man's* problem. It is a solution that solves man's problem by doing away with man.

For in *Being and Time* Heidegger rightly distinguished between ontic and ontological beings, between Angelus Silesius' roses and men, between the life without why and the life of care and concern. But precisely because he was right there, his present relinquishing of what alone distinguishes man from all other beings is a relinquishing of the humanity of man. In *Being and Time* Heidegger counseled facing death as a way of salvation for man. But in his last writings he goes a great deal further and advocates death pure and simple. Since merely facing death but not actually projecting ourselves into this "ultimate possibility" failed to reflect us back into authentic existence, he now advocates that we actually project ourselves into this possibility and commit (moral and intellectual, i.e. human) suicide.

This is, of course, not a new solution. Mysticism, ecstatic religion, and transcendent (rather than transcendental) philosophy have traditionally offered the same advice. But this does not make the advice right and the solution a solution for man.

A true solution can never come from despair, be this a despair in the face of death and nothingness—as in the first stage of Heidegger's hermeneutic—or in the face of the ultimate groundlessness of Being—as in the last stage. It can only come from courageous endurance: an endurance of and in the face of the ultimate groundlessness of Being. Heidegger saw this in *Being and Time,* but, failing to follow up his analysis of man's ontological nature, he failed to show the way to such endurance. Nevertheless, we must find a way if we are to remain human.

It may be true that man is ultimately homeless in the world, that he is by nature "exposed into nothing," and driven to a never ending search for his own Being. But this is no reason for despair; on the contrary, this alone gives us hope and shows us the way to authentic existence. If man's nature is to be ontological, authentic existence does not come from finding a final answer that would put an end to all our questioning; it comes from engaging in the questioning in which our nature is fulfilled. If man is by nature teleological, excellence in living does not come from having reached a final *telos* which would put an end to our teleology (life); it comes from the seeking and striving itself, the fulfilling of our teleological nature. Man may be homeless, ultimately. But he is not ultimately homeless *in the world,* for, as Heidegger shows in *Being and Time,* the world is his home, it is his to make a home of, it is a world only through his home-building, and it is only through his own home-making effort that man can be man and that he can be at home anywhere. In other words man is not just homeless—by nature—he is also a home-maker and thus he can live and abide authentically not by entering into a wholly other abode, prepared and held open for him by a wholly other Being, but by fashioning and making a home for himself out of "ultimately" chaotic materials on an "ultimately" ungrounded ground. This activity alone gives man dignity, for this activity is the source and essence of his life and therefore the home in which he has to dwell.

Heidegger would do well to remember, in his latest writings, the title of his first major work: *Being and Time.* Such a remembering might remind him of the fact that man is a temporal, historical being who lives in time, not in eternity, and therefore needs temporal solutions rather than eternal ones. He needs solutions for the moment in which he lives, solutions from moment to moment as long as he lives, solutions for the innumerable moments that compose his life and history. But these, even the most lasting and satisfactory ones, are finite solutions. And as such they are satisfactory for finite beings whose Being is finite transcendence, a transcendence of the particular limits that define our existence at any moment of its course, rather than a transcendence of finitude as such, a transcendence into infinity and eternity. What man needs in this "time of need" is not the third stage of Heidegger's hermeneutic: the bringing of message and tiding from a wholly other, absolute, and transcendent Being. It is hermeneutic as an interpretation and clarification of finite human existence, the hermeneutic of *Being and Time,* that alone can solve our problems; it is more humanism rather than less that can save, i.e. make essential, human existence.

In his overcoming of metaphysics, Heidegger overextended reason's demand for continued form-giving, defining, de-limiting, and disclosing into a demand for the ultimate and absolute completeness of all definition and disclosure, and thus he ended up with a negative, limiting concept, an empty transcendental idea (of absolutely transcendent Being). In his overcoming of humanistic ethics he overextends the existential, onto-teleological demand of human nature (for continued self-transcendence) into a demand for absolute transcendence, and thus ends up with an empty, totally negative notion of a transcendent existence. He succeeds in overcoming humanistic ethics and attaining to a thinking that is truly beyond good and evil. But, since in this overcoming of humanism not only humanism but the very idea of being human is left behind, the success of Heidegger's nonhumanistic thinking is a dubious, self-defeating victory. Instead of being the triumphant new response to and correspondence with a wholly other Being

that Heidegger aimed at, it is in effect merely the forsaking
of an old and all too human response and responsibility: to
one's own self. As such, it is an irresponsible, infinitely
weary response to the problems of man; it is the feeble
cry of a soul-sick nature that seeks to perish in order
not to perish of its own being. Having accused most
philosophers of nihilism, Heidegger closes his thinking on
a radically nihilistic note.

"Ethics as a mere teaching and exhortation is of no use
unless man first attains to another fundamental relationship
to Being" (*WhD* 34), Heidegger once wrote. But his "other
fundamental relationship" has turned out to be so vague
and directionless as to be no definite relationship at all, to
be, rather, the negation of all relationships, and so Heidegger's demand, that we enter into this new relationship, is
in the end, not even a teaching but just a "mere exhortation" to we know not what. What is the reason for this?

Heidegger's failure is the inevitable result of the basic
shortcoming of all existentialism properly so called: of the
opposition of existence and essence, of life and reason.
Existentialism began as a reaction to an all too barren and
lifeless intellectualism which, in response to the demand
of the intellect for immutability and universality, insisted
on the immutability and universality of all Being and thus
stifled all concern for and movement toward one's own
Being; insisted on the fixity and absoluteness of the Good
and thus stifled all search and striving for one's own good;
insisted on the disclosedness once for all of all Truth and
thus stifled authentic self-disclosure; insisted on irrevocably
fixed and unchangeable essence and thus stifled existence;
insisted on the rule of reason, in and of itself, and thus
stifled life.

As such a reaction and protest, existentialism was a
necessary philosophical movement, a wholesome corrective
to the shortcomings of an all too radical and absolute

rationalism. But unfortunately existentialism remained a mere reaction and a protest, and thus became, in its turn, just as absolute and one-sided as the movement it opposed. Because rationalism insisted on the immutability of truth and Being, existentialism insisted only on historicity, change, and becoming. Because essentialism insisted on the universal, on Law, and on the fixity of all good and value, existentialism insisted only on the unique, opposed all tradition, rule and law, and even refused to think in terms of good and value. Essentialism mistook *nomos*—the particular truths, values, goods, rules, and laws disclosed to man at a particular moment in his historical existence—for *physis* —absolute truths, values, and laws. Existentialism, in its turn, eliminated *physis* and even turned against *nomos,* thus leaving man altogether without guidance, rule, principle, and law. Absolute Idealism pretended to view the world from the point of view of God and arrogated for man the status of Divine Spirit. Existentialism preferred to view the world from the point of view of Abraham trembling in the face of God, and thus arrogated for man no human status, no human dignity, at all.

While such radical opposition (between essentialism and existentialism) is in the end fruitful for philosophy, each of the opposed theories is by itself untenable and self-defeating. At worst each is meaningless, at best each ends as a bitter and impotent preoccupation with, and thus unintended affirmation of, what it seeks to deny. Neither can provide any solution to man's problems, because human existence is not, and thus cannot be understood and clarified as, an either/or proposition (either reason or life, either essence or existence, etc.). Reason in itself, as opposed to the life it has to clarify, disclose, and fulfill, is empty and contentless. Life, without reason, is chaotic and blind. Neither can be or be thought of in their absolute separation. This would be a commonplace hardly worth mentioning except for the fact that, as Heidegger's example shows, it is at times forgotten. But philosophy, if it is to remain philosophy, the love of and search for practical wisdom, cannot forget it, and when it does, as in the case of the late Heidegger, it ceases to be philosophy.

Philosophy cannot be saved by overcoming metaphysics (the thinking about beings), transcending humanism (the preoccupation with man), and going beyond good and evil. It can be saved, or rather kept alive—for no one has quite succeeded in giving it a fatal blow—simply by our engaging in it, if possible, better than, but at least as well as, others have done it before us. Only by keeping it—as metaphysical, humanistic, practical thinking—alive can man—the metaphysical, self-concerned, practical being—hope to keep himself alive in the fullness and richness of his worldly, practical, onto-teleological human existence.

INDEX

Agathon, 58–59, 107–108
Aletheia, 46, 115, 120, 133; as disclosure, 8, 55, 122; of Being, 35, 74, 110, 129, 172; as *a-letheia,* 38, 56; and revelation, 92; in art, 93; as fundamental phenomenon, 106, 132. *See also* Truth
Art, 71–72, 91–105
Authenticity, 10, 130; Dasein when lacking, 17–18, 29–30, gains, 177; and dread, 20; in existence, 186–87, 188, 194; and self-disclosure, 37; and truth, 38; in *BT,* 129, 177–84; and resolve, 179, in the face of death, 182–83, 193; distinguished from the unauthentic, 180–84; compared to *arete,* 181. *See also* Discourse

Beauty, 93–94
Being-in, 18–30
Being-in-the-world: and Dasein, 10, 18, 20, 30, 32, 139; and public conformity, 17; and Discourse, 29

Chre, chrema, 12, 119, 120, 122, 124–25
Correspondence: theory of truth, 33–35, 39, 49; between man and Being, 126–31, 134, 136–38, 141–42, 156–57

Death, 22, 193; being-unto-death, 95, 178–86
Descartes, 42, 48, 60–63, 73, 103
Discourse, 29; as unauthentic articulation, 29, 30, 37

Eckhart, Meister, 152
Ec-sistence, ex-sistence (*Ek-sistenz*), 87–89, 126–28, 130
Ethics, 176–96
Event (*Ereignis*), 110, 155–56
Existence, 5, 9
Existentialism, 196–97
Existentialistic analysis, 5, 6, 9, 27–28

Facticity, 18
Fall (*Verfallenheit*), 29–30
Freedom, 86–90
Fundamental ontology, 3, 5, 9, 77–79

Gelassenheit, 143–46, 149, 151–53, 157, 185
Ground, 147, 151–55, 185, 186

Hegel, 101–103, 161, 166, 174–75; *Phenomenology of Mind,* 102, 137

Heidegger, works of:
Ar, 56;
BT, 1–51, 62–63, 74–85, 87, 88, 126, 128, 129, 139–40, 168, 170, 172, 173, 176–89;
E, 105–06, 139, 169;
ED, 143;
Einf, 23, 59, 93, 94, 95, 97, 101, 106–107, 109, 115, 125, 126;
FD, 53 n., 64–65, 67–68, 79, 175;
G, 15–16, 32, 107, 117, 139, 140;
Gel, 142–46, 156–57, 185, 187;
Holzw, 60, 61–63, 86, 91–105, 137, 139;
Hum, 82, 105, 109, 111–13, 126–31, 139, 163 f.;
Id, 155–56;
KP, 81;
KTh, 67;
N, 26, 60, 68–74, 83, 94–95, 100, 126, 165;
PLW, 52–60;
SG, 65–66, 67, 142, 146–58, 185, 187;
U, 132–36, 138, 141, 143, 184;
Vortr, 22 n., 93, 106, 109, 113, 115, 130, 139, 140;
WhD, 101, 109, 113, 115–25, 138, 139, 166, 168, 196;
WiM, 109–111;
WW, 86–90, 98, 109, 117, 166
Heracleitus, 15, 97, 103, 115, 154
Hermeneutic, 140, 143; in *BT*, 9, 78–79, 177; second stage, 84–85; third stage, 134–36; three stages of, 159–64

Humanism, 28, 53, 59–60, 69–70; *BT* as, 79–81, 176–77, 188; the "overcoming" of, 82–83, 160–65, 189–93, 195, 198; of the later writings, 137–38. *See also* Subjectivism, Metaphysics

Idea, idein, 57–60, 70, 171, 172

Kant, 7, 15–16, 23–25, 31, 46, 63–68, 165–66, 173, 176
Kierkegaard, 89, 186

Language, 29, 111, 130, 132–36, 172–73
Logos, legein, 7, 35, 97, 106, 115–16, 120–24, 132, 189

Mathematical thinking, 62–64, 66; *BT* as, 76, 78–79
Metaphysics: Nietzsche's, 68–70; Heidegger's criticism of, 72–74; *BT* as, 73–82; the "overcoming" of, 82, 159–76
Moira, 113, 140
Mystery, 90, 144, 149, 151–52, 185
Mysticism, 162–64, 193

Nietzsche, 60, 68–74, 140; *Also sprach Zarathustra*, 137 f.
Nihilism, 73, 81–84, 196
Noein, 106, 120–24

Ontology, 3; as a fundamental characteristic of Dasein, 4, 188, 194

Parmenides, 119–25
Phenomenology, in *BT* 6–9, 74–78; reinterpreted, 84–85

Plato, 48, 50, 54–60, 70–73, 101, 103, 140, 165–66, 172, 175; *The Phaedrus,* 94, 101
Possibility, 21; projection of, 23–27, 37; self-projection into, 27, 37

Questioning: as an essential characteristic of man, 3, 5, 9, 188; as unessential for man, 151–54, 158, 191

Reason, rationality, 65, 147–50, 153, 189, 192, 196–97
Resolve (*Entschlossenheit*), 95, 178–83, 185. *See also* Authentic

Sartre, 130 f.
Science, 27–29, 45–46, 143
Spirit, Absolute, 102–103
Subjectivism, 53, 60, 62–63, 66–67. *See also* Humanism

Technology, 74
Teleology, 13, 25, 27, 143, 165, 189, 194

Thought, 103–104, 108–25, 133. See also *Logos*
Transcendence, 154, 169–71, 173–75, 190, 193, 195
Truth: as Dasein's disclosure of Being-in-the-world, 33–43; correspondence theory of, 33–35, 39, 49; criteria and application, 49–51; coherence theory of, 49–50; pragmatic theory of, 50; as correctness, 58; as freedom, 87–90; as the self-disclosure of Being, 89–90, 99–103, 108, 113, 124–25, 131; in art, 92–101; as *physis,* 105; in thought, 112–13, 124–25; and ec-sistence, 126–28; and Being, 128–29; as man-related, 137–38, 141–42, 156–57. See also *Aletheia*

Understanding: in *BT* 20–28; in *SG* 147–48, 153
Utensils and "mere" things (*Zuhandene* and *Vorhandene*), 12–14

World, worldliness, 11–16, 31, 45, 97–98, 194